Praise for

MW00440046

"Aliza Einhorn's very direct and lively way of writing about subjects that often seem overly technical to nonastrologers like myself makes *The Little Book of Saturn* both informative and enjoyable. Anyone who might know just enough astrology to be scared by Saturn's influence or anxious about the (sometimes dreaded) Saturn return, will find this book a helpful friend."

—**Rachel Pollack,** author of
Seventy-Eight Degrees of Wisdom

"For those looking to deepen their knowledge of astrology, I highly recommend Aliza Einhorn's *The Little Book of Saturn*. This may be a little book, but it's big on knowledge! A treat and delight for both seasoned astrologers and those looking to deepen their understanding of the practice, *The Little Book of Saturn* makes astrology accessible, thought-provoking, and fun. Einhorn explains the basics clearly and succinctly, providing an easy entry point into astrology, all while not speaking down to more advanced readers! Einhorn has a knack for making difficult concepts easy to understand. I'd give this book to both beginners and friends who have been casting charts for decades!"

—**Jason Mankey,** author of *The Witch's Book
of Shadows* and *The Witch's Athame*

"Saturn is a harsh teacher, but it is the kind of teacher that, if you can pass its lessons, you come out a stronger, more realized, and autonomous person. If you want the keys to understanding this challenging teacher, *The Little Book of Saturn* is the guide you have been looking for to deepen your under-standing of self and the eternal quest."

—**Adam Sartwell,** cofounder of the Temple
of Witchcraft and award-winning author
of *Twenty-One Days of Reiki* and *The Blessing Cord*

"As a good Capricorn, I have always had a great affinity with Saturn, my ruling planet. Its existence has always given me much curiosity and at the same time a lot of inner peace. Saturn is among the most majestic creatures of the firmament, dressed in its golden tones and sheltered behind a series of perfect rings, made literally from cosmic rocks and stardust. How could one not be curious about it? Finally, someone has taken up the task of recording and supplementing the scarce astrological information previously available about Saturn and delivered it properly broken down and organized in a way that is easy to understand and apply day by day. Finally, Aliza Einhorn's *The Little Book of Saturn* offers the substantial in-formation I have long sought.

"Aliza has given herself the task of creating this incredible book full of effective, comprehensive, and interesting informa-tion based on the astrological spirit of Saturn. This is a more than adequate manual for seekers of stars. From magicians to astrologers and from alchemists to modern sorcerers, every-one should have *The Little Book of Saturn* as an integral part of their collection. It will teach you to understand the different functions of Saturn in your life, in your daily routine, and even the influence it exerts on your zodiac sign. On behalf of all the future readers of this wonderful book, thank you Aliza for this incredible work."

—**Elhoim Leafar,** author of
The Magical Art of Crafting Charm Bags

The Little Book of
SATURN

The Little Book of
SATURN

Astrological Gifts, Challenges, and Returns

ALIZA EINHORN

WEISER BOOKS

This edition first published in 2018 by Weiser Books, an imprint of

Red Wheel/Weiser, LLC
With offices at:
65 Parker Street, Suite 7
Newburyport, MA 01950
www.redwheelweiser.com

ISBN: 978-1-57863-628-0
Library of Congress Control Number: 2018936794

Cover design by Jim Warner
Cover images by Superstock/Julianka and NASA
Interior by Steve Amarillo / Urban Design LLC
Archer Pro and Bodoni BE

Printed in Canada
MAR
10 9 8 7 6 5 4 3 2 1

To my parents, Andrea and Jules

Contents

Acknowledgments

I wish to thank my amazing editor, Judika (my Saturn!), and everyone at Red Wheel/Weiser who was involved in the making of this book.

And to my clients, students, and the remarkable baristas who supported me during the writing and the rewriting, and to dear friends, Amy, Devorah, Kirsten, Lyone, and Tom: I humbly, gratefully thank you.

Introduction:
We Are the Stars

I am so glad you picked up this book. This book wants to be read. This book wants your company.

See, I believe the act of reading is less solitary than we usually think, the reader tugging his or her book (or tablet or phone) out of pocket, purse, or backpack to sneak in a single paragraph or two between the mundane minutes and hours of daily life. I lived in New York City for fifteen years. Deciding what book to take on the subway, no matter the commute, was part of my morning ritual, along with the usual cleansing of the body, and coffee. Whose voice did I need to hear that day? Whose words would be the right words? It's more intimate than not.

Life, my friends, isn't boring, if you are paying attention. There are conversations happening all around you, and the act of reading is a conversation between reader and writer, between reader and book. It matters.

I'm not saying this because I wrote this little book, but because right here, right now, in this introduction, I'm going to tell you something that could change your life. I'm going to tell you the secret of astrology, a secret that not everyone wants to share or believes, but is my perspective as someone who does this for a living, day in and day out.

I am what some would call a consulting astrologer. I do readings for a living, and "reading" in this context means I talk to people about their lives; I help them, using their birth chart as my compass.

Here are a couple of things I want you to keep in mind as we begin to talk:

Astrology Is More than Personality Analysis

You're a Gemini and you're chatty. You're a Taurus and you like plants. Ah, Sun conjunct Venus, how charming you are! Lots of planets in Aquarius? What an original mind you have and oh, oh, oh, Cancer? Bit of a homebody, right?

Yes, part of an astrologer's job is to tell you who you are (and please don't be scared of any unfamiliar terms in this introduction. All will become clear.)

An astrologer looks at your birth chart and can see your personality quirks, your temperament, where the luck is, where the challenge or hardship is, maybe even what you like to eat for breakfast or if you eat breakfast at all.

We see career aptitude, your family, relationship potential, psychological default settings, spiritual longings, desire. We see your beauty. We see what you cannot see.

And more.

What we do not always see is what exactly you will *do* with that quirk, temperament, luck, desire, beauty, challenge, or hardship. That's where your free will comes in (if you believe in free will. Do you?).

I remember my first astrology reading with the man who would become my teacher. He was looking at my chart, staring at this one little section of the wheel. In two seconds flat, he described my core self, what I thought was my core self, which I had always felt ashamed of. Surely it had held me back in life. He singled out the one thing that I felt made *me*, me—although it would be years later, and a different teacher, before I truly saw that poison, my poison, as medicine, before I saw that core self "quirk" as a gift.

But he saw it. He named it. I was hooked. He gave me a reason for why I was the way I was, and it was in the chart.

This is what a natal chart reading is supposed to do: describe you. Describe you well. And any half-way competent astrologer, not to mention the brilliant ones, will pick out qualities you recognize as your own.

Astrologers Predict the Future

Are astrologers fortune-tellers? Prophets? Magicians? Well, it depends on who you ask.

An astrologer's primary tool is the birth chart, otherwise known as the natal chart. We look at it and we say hmmm. We gather information. We say hmmm again. We take notes. We see patterns. We see patterns repeat. We use our intuition (although some, believe it or not, believe intuition has nothing to do with it), and we come to conclusions, such as:

Aha! I see it right here! You will find a good strong healthy relationship (or new home or relief from illness) because of this, this, this, and this here. It's *right here*.

How such a prediction might sound, without translation:

Jupiter will trine your Fifth House ruler while sextile your Seventh House ruler and Pluto opposing your Sun with transiting Pluto through your Fifth House and Saturn trine Venus. See?

With translation? It's in the stars.

Thus, the astrologer's job is:

1. to see

2. to make sense of what they see, put the pieces together

3. to tell it to you in a language you understand

4. to help you move forward or stay in place, it really depends

Astrologers give you the timing—when the future will happen, when more money comes in or more money goes out, for example. Also, there are good, bad, and better days to get married or start a business or get a haircut or go on vacation. Maybe you want to relocate, but aren't sure where. Did you know that there are specific astrology charts for just this purpose?

The bulk of my astrology work is concerned with these everyday decisions and questions, not always dates and times, but looking at where the planets are now and how they are affecting us, and in what way, and what to do about it, if anything.

The hidden truth, however, the secret that I want to tell you, the reason we're here that I alluded to at the start of this introduction, is this:

Astrology can save your life.

Or your marriage.

Or your job.

Or your sanity.

Really. It's that good. Astrology saves you because it prepares you.

I'm sure you know people who have had bad years, bad decades, even, seemingly without a break, painful. Maybe that person is you. And then there are times when life flows, and all is a sweet river. Maybe that person is you too.

Astrology helps you discover. Astrology shows you the life phase or cycle you are currently in and will be in—short term, long term, medium, easy, hard, all of the above—and thus you can learn how to benefit beautifully from the good or easy times and how not to lose hope when the hard moments come. This book is not only an astrology book but also a guidebook to help you through those hard times.

I'm here, not only to teach you astrology essentials without condescension, but also to introduce you to the planet Saturn, which is the focus of this book.

A quick Saturn story:

The first thing I learned about Saturn was fear, that Saturn *is* your fear. X=Y. This is how astrologers talk. Venus is love. Mars is passion. Saturn is fear, and Saturn, I learned, is the place of most resistance in the birth chart. The instinct is to run the other way, to avoid.

I learned astrology when I was in my thirties, in New York City, in an office building on the second floor of a building near Penn Station and St. Francis Catholic Church. I would take the number 3 train, forty-five minutes uptown from my apartment in Crown Heights, Brooklyn. I had come to New York to live what I considered a very traditional Jewish life, but somewhere along the way I did a Google search, and that Google search led me to my first astrology class.

My teacher wasn't like the other ones, the ones who held seminars on Reiki and crystals—not that I don't love Reiki and crystals. My teacher, I later understood, was an occultist, a witch, a tarot reader, and there are things he taught us then that I still don't understand, all these years later.

Week after week, he "went around the wheel," which was a picture he drew with markers on a portable dry-erase board, teaching us the signs and planets and houses, the building blocks of astrology. This was the least we needed to know to begin to understand our own charts and to start interpreting them.

It was usually a small group of students, three or four, sometimes more, for two hours and twenty bucks. After a quick, or not so quick, review of the basics, he would talk about a current transit (which is where the planets are now and the effect they are having on us and our charts), possibly a new moon or full moon, whatever the news was in the sky.

He would then plot the event in a student chart on the dry-erase board as though it were a treasure map and he was finding gold. Sometimes he would spend five minutes on a chart and sometimes forty-five. He made predictions. They often came true.

We learned that each planet has a basic nature, a main keyword or two that describes what it is and what it does. Although keywords sometimes change, especially in the Internet age, when there is more information than we can possible keep track of, the first word I learned for Saturn has stuck with me. Saturn is where *you,* not just the angels, fear to tread. What we dare not approach. Where we hesitate.

And yet we, students of astrology, students of life, must blossom into our charts. One of our jobs in this lifetime is to transform that fear into something else.

This is true of all the planets. We take the raw material and then what? We grow. Years pass. We grow more. In the case of Saturn, we grow into other Saturn keywords which, as you can probably tell, aren't mere keywords at all. From fear to mastery of that fear. From fear to teacher of the things we fear(ed). We wind up far, and yet so close, from where we started. More about this in the chapters ahead.

Saturn, however, is more than fear. Saturn has various associations and images, and I'll discuss many of them in this book. One common Saturn image is of <u>Saturn the teacher, an often strict teacher and giver</u> of life lessons.

My teacher was my Saturn in real life. Make sense? This is how astrology works. Astrology *is* real life. My teacher was a man (which is another Saturn keyword). He was a man older than me (Saturn rules age, maturity). He was a man with knowledge, wisdom, authority. All Saturn keywords. He was Saturn teaching us Saturn.

We Are More than the Stars

Astrology is not just theory or entertainment or a fad to me. It's the way I think. It's the way many of my clients and students think. Astrology is the lens through which we view the world and our lives. Dare I say it's who I am? Well, it's certainly a part of me, part of my cosmology, how I view the world as a semi-grown woman of forty-six, the age I am as I sit here writing to you.

Astrology is how I speak, the language I use to explain a bad day, a bad year, a good day, a good year. Astrology lovers track their lives and experiences, past, present, and future through the movements and meanings of the stars. It does not stop life from happening. If something is meant to be, it will be, but astrology is the best early warning detection system I've ever known.

Dear reader, please know, you do not need any special spiritual or Pagan or astrological knowledge hocus-pocus to read and understand and enjoy this book. You only need to be here.

And now, if you will permit me to be your Saturn, we can begin.

What Is Astrology?

Before we begin our exploration of Saturn, I want to take you on a quick astrological tour, the least you need to know and then some.

Chapter 1

You Are More than Your Sun Sign

Remember life before the World Wide Web? I do. We had books then and newspapers. We listened to music on records, record players. The good old days. And I know, we still have all those things now—there are even two record stores in walking distance from where I'm writing this—but I don't think I'd be mistaken if I said that life was slower before the invention of the Internet. Information was harder to find.

Newspapers and magazines were probably your first exposure to astrology, a daily, weekly, or monthly horoscope. Some of us maybe can't even remember when we first heard the *A* word (astrology) or the *H* word (horoscope) or found out what sign we were. It is like it was always there.

I remember growing up in Miami, Florida, reading my daily horoscope in the *Miami Herald* newspaper. I wondered what those mysterious sentences in that one meager paragraph could possibly mean for me, for my little eight- or nine-year-old life. Whatever age I was, I already knew my Sun sign.

I have another memory, which may be yours as well: the dusty used or discount bookstore full of remaindered books. There was one I used to frequent with my brother on Saturdays in North Miami Beach when my father had us both for the weekend. Among the mysteries and Westerns and crime paperbacks and the *Guinness Book of World Records,* you could also discover a small blue volume by astrologer Linda Goodman, who went Sun sign by Sun sign in thorough fashion. If you were like me, you immediately looked up everyone whose birthday you remembered, comparing and contrasting reality with her written word.

Flash forward to the present day: I admit it. If I were to meet you for the first time, I would wonder when you were born, and I would start guessing, even if only in my mind, secretly.

Underline this point, my dears: your Sun sign absolutely matters, your Sun sign is *you,* but you are more than your Sun.

To understand yourself and to understand everyone else using astrology, you must explore not only the sign the Sun is in but also Moon, Mercury, Venus, Mars, Jupiter, Saturn, Uranus, Neptune, and Pluto. Every one of those planets (we call Sun and Moon "planets" in astrology) is also in one of the twelve signs. For example, we say Pluto in Virgo or Jupiter in Virgo or Venus in Virgo, just as we say Sun in Virgo.

Think of the planets as record albums and the twelve signs as the sleeves they come in. If that's too old school for you, then use the metaphor my astrology teacher often did: the planets as actors and the signs as costumes. The planets change signs as they move around the sky. Some planets move super slow and some move fast. Pluto can spend twenty years in a sign, whereas the Moon will spend two days or so. That's a big difference.

Imagine this: I am meeting you for the first time at a party, and although I'm a cautious Cancer Sun with a reserved Virgo Rising, I can be friendly after a coffee or two, or a glass of Merlot. Trying not to embarrass myself, I pop the question: *When were you born? When's your birthday?*

An astrology chart is like a family, functional, dysfunctional, and everything in between. All the pieces interact. And when I say "astrology chart" or "chart," for our purposes here, I am talking about your birth chart (natal chart), which is determined by your exact birth information including time and date and place. My teacher used to tell us it is a map of the heavens at the time you were born.

We Contain Multitudes

As I've already mentioned, my Sun is in Cancer. My mother, however, was a reserved, secretive Scorpio and we were very close, fused almost. As a kid, anytime I'd read anything about Scorpio, I identified strongly. The first time I had my chart read, in my twenties, I was shocked to discover that I had no planets in this sign. How could this be when I saw myself in every word ever written about Scorpio? But this is normal. To paraphrase Walt Whitman, we contain multitudes.

Although I had no planets in Scorpio, there was a compelling reason for why I felt the way I did. Indeed, there is *something else* in my chart exerting a powerful influence over my mood and personality (and it has to do with the twelve houses, which we will discuss in Chapter Two.) You may also find yourself wondering why you are not such and such Sun sign, when you identify so strongly with it. I promise you there is a reason why you feel like a Leo but your Sun is in Pisces, why you feel like a Libra but your Sun is in Capricorn.

Meet the Family

This book is an introduction to Saturn, but in the spirit of giving you the groundwork, I figure we better meet the whole family, albeit briefly.

Sun

In a birth chart, the Sun is *you*, the core you, the heart of you, the crucial substance of you.

Astrologers may use words like "essence," "ego," "identity," "nature," "purpose." If you read almost any description of Sun in Aries, for example, you should be able to see yourself in it. Brave. Impulsive. Pioneering! Sun in Aries takes initiative. Sun in Aries is bold. Sun in Aries is competitive. You should be able to say, "Yes, that's me," and others will likely see those qualities as well.

I also think of the Sun as what you return to. No matter what happens in your life, no matter what changes and experiences you endure, when everything falls away, you are your Sun. You are you.

Rising Sign

Remember that hypothetical party I mentioned earlier, when I was wondering about your Sun sign? Sometimes I even ask if a person knows their Sun *and* Moon *and* Rising, and if I haven't scared them off, the party really gets going.

The Rising sign is not a planet, but I would argue that it's as important as a planet. The Rising sign is revealed once an astrologer enters your birth information into astrological software, although an "old school" astrologer may still calculate your chart by hand. The Rising sign is literally the constellation that was climbing in the sky, rising in the east, at the time you were born. It is the sign that was ascending and thus the Rising sign is also known as the ascendant.

At that fabulous party, your Rising sign is what's on display. It's how you show up in the world. Your "first handshake" is what astrologers often call it. It's what people see before they get anywhere close to the inner world of your Sun, and yet the Sun always seeks to be seen. The Sun won't hide for long.

You may have an adventurous Sagittarius Sun but a vigilant Scorpio Rising. Folks will no doubt pick up on that Scorpio Rising reserve *first* and then, after a conversation or two, if they are perceptive, they will get a glimpse into the core daredevil Sagittarius you.

Moon

The Moon in your chart symbolizes your feelings, your emotional life, including what you need to feel safe or nurtured. Habits, instincts, and gut reactions also fall under the domain of the Moon. The Moon is how you respond to what happens.

A more demonstrative Moon (often a water or fire sign) will feel first and think later. Feelings may rise up on the inside like a pot of water boiling over.

A more intellectual moon may "think" their feelings first: *What is this? What do these feelings mean?* They often seem detached to the more "emotional" Moon signs. Signs who have a tendency to analyze, like Gemini, an air sign, or Virgo, an earth sign, may not even know what they feel because they are already onto the next thing in their minds. Feelings tend to stick around, though, in the body, whether or not we stay aware of their presence.

The Moon shows what can help you self-soothe. The Virgo Moon needs a plan and then can relax. Cancer Moon needs a mother or a mother stand-in, some nurturing, and something sweet. Taurus Moon may require just the sweet or some other edible or physical creature comfort, a favorite blanket or sweater, for example. Moon in Sagittarius needs to feel free. Moon in Capricorn or Scorpio needs to brood. Each Moon, like all the planets, behave according to the sign they "wear."

Mercury

Mercury is your mind, how you think and speak. Your Mercury shows whether your thoughts are clear and logical or muddy and murky. Are you a poet or a politician or both? Your Mercury will show it.

Mercury in the fire signs (Aries, Leo, Sagittarius) tend to be confident in their opinions, or at the very least, they speak their minds.

Mercury in one of the water signs (Cancer, Scorpio, Pisces) may be just as confident or quick but will express their deep thoughts literally more quietly, or not at all, keeping thoughts hidden.

Mercury in one of the air signs (Gemini, Libra, Aquarius) tend to be friendly and cerebral, and they may have trouble relating to emotional swings.

Mercury in one of the earth signs (Taurus, Virgo, Capricorn) will give you helpful, practical, no-nonsense, commonsense advice.

Venus

Venus is the love nature: what you love, how you love. It represents your taste, not just in romantic relationships, but also in the things of this world.

When we want to see if love is coming or we want to see your romantic history, we astrologers ask Venus. If we want to see your ability to give and receive love, we ask Venus. Are you a monk or a serial monogamist? Can you mate for life? Ask Venus. Do you draw people to you or do you push them away? Venus!

Mars

Mars is your energy, drive, passion, what gets you up and going in the morning (or not). What motivates you? Ask Mars. What makes you angry? Ask Mars. What pushes you to act? Ask Mars! Mars fights. Mars competes. Mars wants to do it.

Venus and Mars are the planets astrologers associate most with love and desire and sex. I believe both planets can show our self-worth and our courage, even though Venus tends to get lumped in the self-worth/self-esteem category, and Mars is more often associated with raw power and sexuality.

Venus wants passion and sex just as much as Mars does, but her style, at its most valued, is indirect, like flirtation, for example. A skilled Venus lets you know what she wants with a beautiful gesture, unlike Mars's huff and puff and grunt.

Fast, Slow, and Maybe Medium

The planets that I just described above—Sun, Moon, Mercury, Venus, and Mars—are often called the personal or inner planets, and they have an obvious influence on our personalities. These personal planets move quickly around the sky, and their influence is short term when by transit. *Transits are where the planets are now and how they affect us.*

When your astrology-loving friend is complaining about his Moon transit, the good news is that it will likely last just a couple of hours, compared to other transits that can last months or even years. Although damage and destruction can happen in a heartbeat (speaking as someone who has survived hurricanes in both Florida and New York), I find it reassuring to know when a storm is a fast-moving one.

Everything in the chart is interconnected. We have these fast-moving personal or inner planets, and we also have slower-moving, generational planets.

Astrologers called these planets generational because everyone born in such-and-such year will have Jupiter in a certain sign, or everyone born over a twenty-year period will have Pluto in a particular sign. Some astrologers see Jupiter and Saturn as connecting the fast movers and slow movers because they fall somewhere in the middle. Call them medium movers if you want, but to keep things simple and clear, I'm creating just the two columns for us, fast and slow.

Also, I lied. I actually do have a planet in Scorpio, but I didn't want to mention it until we got to this part of the chapter about generational planets. I am part of Generation Neptune in Scorpio. You, reading this, may share my Neptune, or you may have your Neptune in Libra or Sagittarius or another sign.

The Outer Planets

Jupiter changes signs once a year and represents opportunity, growth, luck, blessing, and abundance. Good things happening. "Jupiter expands what it touches" is a common key phrase. I like to say that Jupiter makes things big. Excess. Inflation. The potential problem with Jupiter is too much of a good thing.

Saturn stays in a sign around two-and-a-half years. It represents structure, maturity, and the reality check. Saturn *shapes*. More about Saturn in the pages to come.

Uranus changes signs every seven years. The planet of surprise. The wild card. Uranus is original, inventive, innovative, and often just plain weird. "Expect the unexpected" is what they say. Uranus sets you free, whether you want it or not. Uranus shatters.

Neptune will change signs every fourteen years and is associated with art, spirituality, mysticism, and self-sacrifice. My teacher used to say Neptune is "illusion, delusion, confusion." Neptune is the fog. We see what we want to see when Neptune is in town, and it may look amazing. Neptune goggles. Glamour. You will not see clearly under Neptune. Things may appear better *or* worse than they truly are. Neptune conceals and ideals.

Pluto is our slowest mover and may spend twenty-five years in a single sign. Pluto energy is intense, magnetic, and is associated with power, death and rebirth, obsession and compulsion, sex, taboo, and the underworld. On a good day, Pluto can heal you because it forces you to go deep and get to the root of the matter of what hurts. Pluto is psychic. On a bad day, Pluto is criminal, manipulating you because she or he can. Pluto transits are the most comprehensive, transformative, and life changing.

Planets in
Signs in Houses

I do not remember when I first learned to think like an astrologer. I think it came naturally to me, the language, the symbols. Whatever it was, I liked it. Astrology seemed to explain almost everything, and what it didn't explain was a mystery to explore and uncover.

In Chapter One, I introduced to you the idea of planets wearing clothes and the popular metaphor that my teacher liked, the planets as actors and the twelve signs as their costumes: Sun in Aries, Moon in Taurus, Mercury in Gemini, and so forth.

There is no naked planet, my friends; the planets are always getting dressed. Sun in Scorpio is not the same as Sun in Gemini and not the same as Sun in Capricorn. The twelve signs lend their particular quirks and poetry to each planet, and each planet, along with the Rising Sign, represents another part of you, from your emotions to your brains to your guts to your deepest, most private self.

On Timing, Which Is Also a Saturn Topic

If you were born in the spring, you are not a Virgo. Virgo is a late summer, early fall sign. If you were born in late summer, you are not a Capricorn. Capricorn is winter. You'll see in a moment where I'm going with this.

I have no idea *when* you are reading this book, but you know. You can connect to what time it is. It's all around you. It is there in the weather and the holidays and the clothing and the office parties and simply the feeling in the air. That fall smell, that summer smell, that spring smell. Does winter have a smell? I believe it does.

It is late November as I am writing, and soon to be December in Florida, where I live now. The Sun entered Sagittarius just a few days ago. The Sun is wearing a new costume and our consciousness has shifted from the imagery and affairs of Scorpio to the imagery and affairs of Sagittarius.

During the seasons of Sagittarius and Capricorn, we have festivals of light and hope from various cultures—think Christmas, Chanukah, Diwali, to name just three—whereas during Scorpio time, we have Halloween, the Day of the Dead, the Feast of All Saints, Samhain, all far darker in feeling and design. After the dark comes light. After death comes birth or rebirth. Make sense? What time is it where you are?

Each moment and time of year is unique, distinct, and at each moment there is another soul born, another soul reflecting the sky. I have no idea what season, what month, what time of day it is for you, right now, this moment, but I want you to feel it. Tune in.

Let's Talk about the Houses

The astrological wheel is divided into twelve parts that we call the houses. Each house is associated with a sign and a planet.

The houses are the areas of life, *where* things happen and *what* things happen to you, such as your job, health, relationships, family, spiritual life, love, and more.

Why are the houses important?

You don't just have your Sun in Aquarius or your Venus in Taurus. Your Sun and Venus and each of your planets is located *somewhere* in your chart, in one of those twelve sections, and this somewhere, obviously, has meaning.

Remember this, if you want to think like an astrologer: It's a set number of pieces that we're playing with here—planets, signs, houses. Forever and ever these pieces overlap and interlock and weave together, and thus the richness of interpretation of a natal chart is born. How you—yes, you—put it all together is the magic. If you dare.

Here's an example:

You may have your Sun in sensitive water sign Cancer, but it lies in the house that is associated with daredevil fire sign Sagittarius. Water plus fire. You can see how this would be different than, say, Sun in Cancer in the watery Scorpio house. Water and water tend to get along. Same element. Compatible. Emotional.

But water and fire? Hmm. Sun in Cancer in the Ninth House (which is the Sagittarius house) may not get along with herself!

A "typical" Sun in Cancer may be introverted, whereas many Sagittarians tend to be extroverted. Private versus public. Homebody versus where's the fun? How do you think this overlap would affect her personality or expression of her Cancerian-ness?

Now of course not *all* Cancer Suns are introverts and not *all* Sagittarius are extroverted, but let's continue.

Another example:

You may hear your astrology-loving friend say, "Oh yes, I'm a Taurus Sun, *but* my Taurus Sun is in the Twelfth House, so I hoard only meditation cushions." Taureans tend to be collectors and savers, and the Twelfth House is one of the more spiritual houses where a collection of meditation cushions would feel at home.

More Overlap, Empty Houses, and
Keywords, Keywords, Keywords

Let's say you meet someone at a groovy party, and let's say this someone knows their chart pretty well, and you want to know them, and you are a beginning student of astrology, and maybe you own this book and you are following along, and this person is smart enough to tell you that their planet X is in sign Y in house Z. Even without knowing anything else, with this information, you will know a lot.

Let's say they tell you that they have their Sun in Gemini in the Eighth House.

This person may have a lot to say on the topics of sex or the occult (common Eighth House concerns). Sun in Gemini loves information and tends to be social. A Sun in Gemini in the Eighth House, however, may be more private or secretive, or simply talk about Eighth House topics or be obsessed with Eighth House topics.

Do you see what I'm doing here? Notice the overlap? Having this planet/sign/house formula gives you a hotline to knowing who someone is.

Wherever the Sun is placed (as with all the planets), the things of that house will be in the life.

The house will show areas of focus or concern or love or struggle or preoccupation. The meaning of "empty houses," houses where you have no planets at all, is subject to debate, as is so much of astrology (astrologers are like rabbis, often disagreeing), and I can only briefly touch on this complex subject here. This question came up in one of my classes the other day so it's on my mind. My student said: "I have nothing in my Fifth, Sixth, and Seventh Houses. What does it mean?"

Does the empty house create a feeling of lack? Or that the matters of that house are already solved and do not need further attention in this lifetime? I recommend learning how to read your own chart, of course, and answering this question for yourself. Your life will tell you.

Learning how to think like an astrologer also includes keywords, lots of them, and I think the more you know, the better. It's not like cooking. If you're making fettuccine Alfredo, you don't throw everything in. There's a recipe. With astrological keywords, be a glutton. Start with the most common (for planet, sign, and house) and then discover more traditional or arcane or less common, more interesting ones.

Eventually there will come a day, and you're at that party, and someone is telling you that they have their Sun or Moon in Taurus in the Fifth House, and you will give them your own personal creative intuitive astrological point of view.

Your birth chart shows your uniqueness, and honestly, it doesn't matter whether you want to read anyone else's chart. If you picked up this book, then you likely want to read, understand your own. You want to read, understand, yourself.

House by House

The First House is your personality, associated with Aries and Mars. The Rising sign (Ascendant) is found here. The First House may show your appearance and also your health. The First House is what others see when they see you.

The Second House is your stuff, your money, your earnings, associated with Taurus and Venus and what you value. Also, self-worth. I call it one of the work houses, along with the Sixth and the Tenth.

The Third House is aligned with brainy Mercury and Gemini, and thus symbolizes communication and the way you think, your perception, but also short-distance trips, your environment and neighbors, and contracts too.

The Fourth House is home, your current home and the one you come from, family, associated with Cancer and the Moon. It is one half of the parental axis. Depending on which astrologer you ask, it represents the mother or father. When you look at your chart dead on, this house is at the bottom, and astrologers give it extra importance (along with the First, Seventh, and Tenth).

The Fifth House is fun and kids, associated with Leo and the Sun, creativity, self-expression. I call this one of the love houses, along with the Seventh and Eighth, and I do use the word "love" liberally here. The Fifth House tends to be associated with love affairs and dating as opposed to committed relationships, but we all have to start somewhere. This house is more private than the Eleventh, which opposes it (lies opposite) on the wheel.

The Sixth House is associated with Virgo and Mercury and is the house of service, servants, and help. It's a health house too. I look here first when I want to see how your health is. It's also the house of work—not career with a capital *C* (that's the Tenth House), but your daily duties and routines.

The Seventh House is committed partnerships, marriage, and is associated with Libra and Venus. Another one of the love houses but can reflect your clients or very close friends. It is opposite the First House, and whereas the First House is *you,* the Seventh House is *not you.* First House is *me.* Seventh House is *we.* It's the person you think you're not. I look to this house to see the status of your relationship or lack of one.

The Eighth House is associated with Scorpio and Pluto and our dark deep hidden desires and motives, sex and death and rebirth and the occult, our deepest intimacies with others. It is one of the spooky houses, along with the Twelfth House that folks may have trouble understanding or be frightened of because the associations are so primal. Also known as the house of other people's money (as opposed to the Second, which tends to be your own earnings).

The Ninth House rules religion, publishing, broadcasting, the law, long-distance travel, teaching, and preaching. Associated with Sagittarius and Jupiter, this house represents your perspective after the intensity of the Eighth House. It's the light of day after the Eighth House's darkness.

The Tenth House is the other half of the parental axis, father or mother. Associated with Saturn and Capricorn, this is where we get clues about your career and ambition. Also the house of status and fame, how others think about you, reputation. Notice that the opposing house is the house of *home*.

The Eleventh House is Aquarius and Uranus and is associated with your friends, networks of people, groups you belong to or want to belong to. Also, "fondest hopes and dreams," as my teacher used to say. Difficult planets here can make friendship hard to sustain. If you have a few planets here, then you probably have a lot of dreams and goals.

The Twelfth House is another spooky house. Associated with Pisces and Neptune, here we find, on a bad day, self-sabotaging behaviors and addiction, escapism, prisons. On a good day, it's the monk on the mountain, meditating, feeling at one and at peace with all that is, spirituality and mysticism and love which has no bounds. Also, clues to your mental health can be found here.

Wise and Patient Saturn

Our focus must shift now as we step away from general astrology to Saturn. The four chapters that make up this section explore a few of Saturn's facets and functions, like a god or goddess with many names.

Who Is Saturn?

So who is this Saturn, anyway? So important that he commands his own book! What does Saturn symbolize in the horoscope? And what does he want from us?

Although symbolism and meaning will sometimes overlap from planet to planet, each planet has its own distinct vocabulary and flavor. Saturn is no different. If I had to pick a flavor, I would say Saturn is sour, not sweet. Cold, not hot. Matter-of-fact, not passionate. And if I had to describe the keywords that best fit Saturn, I'd say that they were tough and hard keywords. Unforgiving words. Serious words. Make sense?

Unlike graceful Venus, Saturn is not a softy. Unlike fast-paced Mars, Saturn is slow moving, not in a hurry. Unlike buoyant Jupiter, Saturn is the realist of the zodiac, not the fun-loving cheerleader.

Saturn's themes and words and flavors are like a map that show you what you *need* to do for yourself and for other people in this life, which is different than what you want to do. Saturn symbolism is rife with the "have to's" of existence, such as homework, your job, having patience, taking responsibility, managing your health and money, aging, even death. Commitments of all kinds.

More often than not, Saturn tells you where you are going wrong in this life, not where you are going right. He's our cosmic alarm clock, forever going off on a Saturday or Sunday at six a.m. when you would rather sleep in. Wake up, says Saturn! Get up! Don't be late! Saturn won't lie to you or gossip or tell tall tales. Saturn won't make a promise without keeping it. Saturn means business. Saturn comes through. Saturn is the reliable one, dedicated and responsible.

If you want to dream, go to Neptune. If you want to write the perfect blog post, see Mercury. If you want to do better at being in touch with your feelings, visit your natal Moon. If you want a wake-up call? If you want a reality check? If you want to know your life purpose? Get to know your Saturn.

Let's break it down a bit more to some of Saturn's main themes.

Saturn Is Your Fear

The first word I ever learned for Saturn, what Saturn symbolized in the horoscope, was the word "fear," that in our birth charts, Saturn represents a kind of mental or emotional or even physical blockage in our psyches. Something we can't do. Something we won't do. We stop. We freeze. We avoid. And not only do we feel this fear, but we feel bad for feeling it. Inadequate. Somehow we just don't measure up and we know it, we feel it, even if we don't know why or can't quite pinpoint what it's all about.

Questions: What are we afraid of? What are we avoiding? Answer: the particular qualities and characteristics and destiny of whatever sign our Saturn is in, in our birth charts. The things of that sign will feel impossible to us, even forbidden, something that we'll never ever have no matter how much we long for it.

The fact that Saturn is in a particular sign in our birth charts shows us that that sign, like the sign of our Sun or Mercury or Moon, and the other planets, is a part of us. Saturn, however, by its very nature creates this seemingly insurmountable fear in us, which leads us to feeling trapped, restricted, constricted. How can we ever get what we want with this Saturn in the way?

This is why knowing your Saturn sign is so important—so that you can get to know your fear inside and out. So that you can study your fear up close and personal, smell its breath on you. Saturn won't be satisfied with us just "knowing" and sniffing our fears, no matter how up close we are. Saturn will push us to confront the fears and to get over them, and the only way to do this is through life experience, through making mistakes. For Saturn, it's not enough to think or analyze or dream or wonder about the future. Saturn wants us to plan. Saturn will give us lesson after lesson, test after test, challenge after challenge, from birth until we draw our last breath, all in the service of transforming our fears into fearlessness.

Saturn, as our fear, feels like a wall or mountain we cannot scale, cannot climb. It's too high, too thick, too broad. It's probably covered in thorns and barbed wire and bad smells and bad people and every possible impediment. I am trying to create an extreme picture here because Saturn *is* extreme, extreme fear, extreme feeling of restriction and constriction, and if any one of us dare face even an eighth of our Saturn fears, then we have accomplished much in this lifetime.

You may have little awareness that the locus of your fears has a name (Aries, Taurus, Cancer, or one of the other signs), that your fears have a vocabulary and a flavor and a planet in charge of it, and a particular energy and pages of keywords that can be referenced. You may think, "Oh, this is who I am, and I will live with my fears without challenging them or trying to climb that wall out of the fear place." But once you know the astrology, there's no turning back. Once you know your own chart, you will grasp what Saturn in Aries or Gemini or Libra or Scorpio means for you and how that wall of fear can be dismantled brick by brick by brick.

Saturn Is Your Work

Every planet, including Saturn, has both positive and negative keywords and symbolism, ideas that feel good to us and ones that don't. Saturn as our fear obviously gets put in the "negative" column of the ledger. No one wants to feel afraid. It's unpleasant, to say the least. We would rather come into this world all brave and strong and smiling, ready to make our beds and greet the day. Although Saturn is a serious planet, there are Saturn manifestations that actually are fun to explore and talk about. It's not all gloom and doom.

One of these is Saturn as our work, but it's work on a few different levels.

The first level of work is how we usually think about it, your job itself and the field you're working in. Medical? Law? Business? Art? Teaching? Healing? Service industry? Not sure? Self-employed? Corporate? It's not an accident that you are in your current job, and it's not an accident if you leave that job for one that better suits you. I promise that your natal Saturn and the sign it's in had something to do with your choices.

No doubt you felt drawn to what you do, but if you are in touch with your Saturn, even a little, you may also have felt daunted or afraid. Because of this Saturn fear, it could take years, even decades, for you to find the position that fits you best. That Saturn hesitation will create delays.

Saturn also represents both discipline and structure in the horoscope, and without these key principles, you won't go to work, you can't go to work. You have to get up on time. You have to catch your train or put gas in the car. You have to do what they want you to do. Follow the rules! You probably have a boss or maybe you are your own boss, but without discipline and structure, work falls apart.

The second level of Saturn work is how far you will go in your job, how high up you want to climb. Keyword: achievement. Saturn helps you figure out how ambitious you actually are; this is the moment when that word "job" becomes "career," and you ponder where you are and where you want to be. Saturn rules ambition and status, awards and honors. The difference between a Saturn job and a non-Saturn job is that the non-Saturn job could disappear tomorrow and you'd be fine, but with the Saturn job? You care. Also, you have a reputation to protect. Someone in touch with their mature Saturn self will want to find that right career, keep climbing, and not give up.

The third level of Saturn work is what you are meant to do in this lifetime, your "life's work," which may be more than your daily job or even what you consider your career. You may pay the bills by teaching, but your life path is to be a mother. You may be the CEO of a company, but your life work is animal communication. For some of you, the job or career and life path will dovetail.

Saturn asks: What is your life purpose? This too is your work, to know the answers to these questions. Why were you born? Why are you here? More work, more questions to answer—but this is work of the spirit as well as the hands. Also, this is when words like "fate" and "karma" usually show up in the Saturn conversation. Saturn doesn't believe in random. Saturn doesn't believe in chaos. Saturn believes in the plan, the form, the structure, and that we all have a specific, unique life purpose. Saturn in your birth chart will absolutely give you clues to all of these—your job, career, ambition, and larger fated destiny.

Saturn in his wisdom and patience requires that we go slow and don't skip steps in our rise to the top of the work or career mountain, whichever mountain we happen to choose to climb. We will get Saturn Returns along with other Saturn transits. These transits make us pause, reflect, reevaluate where we are and what we need to do next so that we build up slowly. Saturn will not be satisfied with some impulsive, half-cocked decision-making process. Taking your time is advised, says Saturn.

Saturn Is Your Duty

To whom are you obligated? To what? Saturn is your fear, your work, and also your duty. Saturn is what you feel you must do. Whether you call it duty or obligation or commitment or a promise you cannot break, one of Saturn's jobs is to make sure you keep your word. Saturn will make you feel guilty if you don't.

Here's an example: It's not unusual to find "Saturn people" in the military or armed forces across the nations. Four-star generals, even. And by Saturn people, I mean Capricorn Risings, or Capricorn Suns and Moons, or someone who has many planets in Capricorn in their birth chart. They are good at being in charge *and* at following direction. They respect the rules! Remember that Saturn is the planetary ruler of the sign of Capricorn.

A Saturn person could also be someone with a prominent Saturn in his or her birth chart, no matter their Sun or Moon or Rising signs. Their Saturn may literally be at the top of their chart or in one of the more important houses, like the First House.

Saturn is at home with law and order and discipline, so the military is a natural fit for these Saturn types. Saturn people make the best soldiers because they will not abandon their troops, no matter the risk. You will also see Saturn people in law enforcement and first-responder fields. Protect and serve!

Where Saturn is placed in your chart is how you will discover where your duty lies. Saturn rules honor. We are not all born to be decorated military men or women, so this sense of commitment or duty will show up in other ways. We all feel obligated to something or someone, even if that someone is ourselves.

You can observe the duty to family in the father or mother who works three jobs to support the kids, making sure they have everything they need. This is also the one who is taking care of their sick or aging parents or grandparents. It's the father or mother who is caring for their grandchildren, feeding and clothing and loving. Many of us consider our pets family and I have known more than one cat lady or cat man who felt obligated to feed the stray or feral cats in the neighborhood or rescue these animals when neglect or abuse was indicated.

Saturn is not about choice. The woman who rescues a neglected dog is not making a choice. The man who cares for his ninety-year-old grand-mother is not making a choice. The sense of duty is bigger and stronger and bloodier than choice. It's a requirement, and you can see the strength of some-one's Saturn in their behavior.

This is something I will tell you over and over, that Saturn is in the *doing*. Saturn is not about how you feel. It's not about ideas. If you feel obli-gated or committed to someone or something, then you aren't going to sit around and think about it. Instead, you are going to get up. You are going to work for your family, your community, your coun-try, your world.

You may feel duty toward your boss, your career, your life path. You may feel it's your duty to expand your self-awareness and spirituality. You may be a teacher and feel obligated to teach your students everything you know. You may feel committed to your neighborhood, cleaning up stray garbage or volunteering in a senior center or helping kids at risk. For you, it may play out more personally, and your biggest commitment is to your child. For others, it's global, and they discover themselves committed to an idea, like a political belief.

As you can see, this duty can play out in all kinds of ways, but one thing is certain: If you are here on this Earth, then you have a birth chart and you have a Saturn, and that Saturn is somewhere, and that somewhere determines where and how and when you feel obligated and loyal, be it to a person or a cause. Saturn is a protector, guardian, shepherd, and what we feel we must protect will vary from person to person. Your chart holds the key.

Saturn Is Your Growing Up

Saturn is the principle of growing up and growing older. Saturn symbolizes aging and time. Father Time is Father Saturn.

Saturn does not let us stay flailing in childhood or young adulthood a moment later than we need to. We must learn how to tie our shoes, pay our bills, learn the proper way to boil an egg, to handle difficult people. Or maybe we ourselves are the difficult ones. We have to learn these skills, learn the rules of life, what to do and how to do it in order to best survive. Saturn doesn't want us to be taken care of. Saturn wants us to fend for ourselves. And many of us still don't know how to act our age, despite our human years. Finally, I've learned how to make the perfect hard-boiled egg, although I always have to look up the instructions. Good enough, says Saturn!

The first Saturn Return comes around age twenty-eight (see Chapter 6 for more on this), and then if we live long enough, we get two more. Each Saturn Return is a bridge to another world, a world called More Knowledge with its capital city, More Work. Whether you use a romantic word like "bridge" or "gate," or a witchy word like "crossroads" or "portal," one thing is clear. With each year, Saturn has more to teach us, and yet the lessons are eerily the same: Grow up!

When I was a kid, or even as an adult, "immature" was one of the worst things you could call someone. It certainly is from Saturn's point of view. Don't be a baby, says Saturn at his meanest. You want to make Saturn angry? Do something you would have done ten or even twenty years ago and then cry about it. But what does it really mean to grow up?

One word: responsibility. Saturn requires we take responsibility for who we are, what we say, what we do. It's just what grown-ups do.

Saturn also prefers we make wiser and more mature decisions as we go, but no matter what we choose, Saturn as the grow-up principle is all about not blaming others for our mistakes or our successes. If we did it, then we must own it. We may not like it, and we may feel ashamed or guilty. We may have chosen wrongly. I know I have. But we are our behavior, says Saturn. We are our actions. And that is the key to growing up: responsibility and accountability.

Wisdom, however, is more than "mere" growing up and is another Saturn keyword related to aging and time. It's where we are ultimately supposed to get to with Saturn. It's the last stop on the Saturn train. Wisdom is more than logic and more than intuition and emotional IQ. It's a combination of these plus your years on this planet.

Wisdom is the result of everything you've seen and done, experienced, witnessed. You've learned from everything Saturn had to teach you and now, only now, you can teach others. Saturn represents this stretch of land from immaturity and childhood to mastery of our fears, of our life path, of our duty, of our growing up.

How Saturn Shows Up in Our Lives

Saturn isn't just a group of keywords or abstract ideas. Saturn shows up in our lives as actual people, usually as authority figures and experts of various kinds at various levels. Here are some of them from real life.

Saturn the Teacher

Is there ever an age when we do not have a teacher? Often the first place we encounter Saturn the teacher is in the classroom when we are children, but teachers and teaching moments are all around us all the time. You may be one yourself!

I can still remember some of the teachers that I had when I was in nursery school. I remember their names, the clothing they wore, their hairstyles, whether they were nice or not so nice. These memories have stuck with me even if I cannot recall most of what I was taught back then—although I do remember clearly the day I learned that 5 + 5 = 10, and the bright black and red picture of ten ladybugs in my workbook. It was a teacher who gave me that workbook, and a pencil, and taught me the mostly forgotten lessons inside it. Teachers tell us the rules (or in some circumstances, make us guess the rules), and it is our job to follow these rules, often with no questions asked. We aren't supposed to make up our own.

The rules exist, says Saturn, to keep order in the classroom and to make organized learning possible. If everyone did what they wanted, there would be chaos. Class starts at a particular time. Class ends at a particular time. Raise your hand to ask a question. Raise your hand to give an answer. Raise your hand to go to the bathroom. Teachers create the lesson plans. Teachers give the homework. Teacher and student are not the same, Saturn says. In the classroom, not everyone can be in charge. We can't all be the teacher.

Of course, there are teachers outside the classroom too, mentors and guides of all kinds, but when Saturn shows up as teacher, know this: He or she has specific knowledge and experience to share with you. It's your job to listen, pay attention, and assimilate the information. There likely will be homework assignments to do. Getting straight As is not a given; if you don't show up to class, then you likely won't pass the class. Lateness will not be tolerated. Rules, rules, and more rules.

I wonder how many of you experienced the very domineering Saturn type of teacher versus the more loving teacher type. I had both growing up. I preferred the soft-spoken ones and was scared of the enforcers, but both can be Saturn. Saturn the teacher doesn't have to be mean to make the rules and set the pace and keep the order. You can rule with a gentle hand. If you are a teacher, then you get to make this choice. You can be a gentle giant or a terrible tyrant. Also, Saturn the teacher not only expects but requires respect because without respect, without obedience, the teacher cannot teach.

Now, because Saturn is always an authority figure, he or she is positioned as knowing more than us and what is best for us, having power over us, no matter our age. How you feel about this, how you feel about Saturn and authority figures, is determined by your own Saturn in your own chart! You may be comfortable with authority or you may be uncomfortable. Some people are fine with others having power over them, and some will rebel in one form or another.

Which type of teacher would you be? Which type of student?

Saturn the Father

Another way that Saturn shows up in our lives is when Saturn shows up as father. This is the parent who is the head of the family, but more than the head, he is the disciplinarian of the family, the god of the family. He is the one who creates the family rule, the family law, what is permitted and what isn't in terms of proper behavior: how to act, how to speak. He will likely set the bedtimes and even enforce the dress code. That shirt? Too tight! Those shorts? Too baggy!

These rules always exist, whether they are spoken or unspoken. Saturn the father is also the one who delivers the punishment if punishment is to be given. He may also decide what the punishment should be, in addition to carrying it out. Saturn the father is the bringer of fate to the children and possibly even to the spouse.

Now, Saturn the father may literally be the mother or other relative; the gender doesn't matter here. Saturn the father can be male or female, even though Saturn is often characterized as male, and even I refer to Saturn as "he" in this book.

Regardless of gender, Saturn the father is someone who had a hand in raising you and may have been the one to take a hand to you. He's the one you have to answer when you've done wrong or fear you've done wrong. No point in lying about it! Somehow, they always know. Saturn the father is tough love.

Saturn the father is more than punishment, though, more than godlike stature to be revered and feared. To father someone is to guide them, to show them the ropes, the skills one needs for life, which can be done in a brutal way or a calm and gentle way. One of Saturn's jobs in the family is to help prepare the child, teach the boy to be a man and the girl to be a woman.

You don't have to be harsh to be Saturn the father, and yet it's a different energy altogether than the stereotypical hug of love we associate with mother energy. If you did not have a father in your life, or a fathering influence, then there are key lessons that you missed. You must learn them in other ways. You must find this knowledge elsewhere.

"Father" is also a synonym for "creator" or "inventor," so here we have this person who helped create you or raise you and then continues to mold you into the person he or she wants you to be. They father you by showing you the way.

Saturn the Leader

Saturn will also show up in our lives as the community leader, the one in charge of the group. These Saturn figures have an exceptionally high level of expertise and experience in their domains, and they likely have people below them, subordinates, as well as a Saturn figure that they themselves must answer to.

One example of this is the spiritual leader, like a Catholic priest, a rabbi, a shaman, a Wiccan priestess. In these roles, Saturn as leader exists to serve the larger community (rather than just a family or classroom), whatever the religion or spiritual discipline. Even in my nondenominational meditation class, which was open to the public, our facilitator was our spiritual Saturn. He taught us meditation techniques from all around the globe. He created the structure for our class, and there were rules to follow: when to sit, when to stand, when to be quiet, when to meditate. He was more than "just a teacher" to us, imparting information and giving wisdom for the week. He was our brave leader, and we recognized his Saturn-ness even if he didn't, which is actually another key Saturn quality: humility.

Spiritual leaders of the major organized religions have even more responsibilities and influence than one local meditation teacher. How should holidays be celebrated? What prayer book should be used? What prayers are best for which occasions? What foods are permitted to eat and when? Whom are we allowed to marry? What are the most important rituals? How do we bury the dead? These questions must have answers that are easy for the laypeople to understand, and every spiritual community in every city will likely have its own customs as well as customs that all practitioners share. It's the spiritual Saturn leaders who decide for the people what to do, when to do it, and what matters most. Saturn decides the rules so that we don't have to. Most people don't want this job. Most people don't want to be Saturn.

The pope is a perfect example of Saturn as community and spiritual leader. He is the face, heart, and soul of the Catholic Church. He is the one who sets the tone for Catholics today, giving talks and sermons from the Vatican. At the same time, he is beholden to tradition, to custom, to law. This is also Saturn. The pope can't just do whatever he feels like, whenever he wants. He is Saturn, but he also answers to Saturn.

I have a friend in New York City who must ask her *rav,* which is a rabbi with specialized knowledge in a certain area of Jewish law, every time she has a question about kashrut, the rules of keeping kosher (Jewish dietary laws). Even though she is an Orthodox religious woman and well versed in the basics, questions inevitably still arise, and they have to talk it out. He's her Saturn in these matters even if she's the Saturn at home with her family.

How else does Saturn show up as a leader? Another example is politics, be they world leaders or at the local level. A president or prime minister is Saturn, and President Saturn is surrounded by all the other Saturns, who have varying degrees of power and authority. In the United States, at the top of the mountain, we have the president, vice president, attorney general, secretary of state, the heads of the FBI and CIA, and more. Each commands their own little, or not so little, slice of Washington, DC.

Saturn Is Everyone

Anyone can be your Saturn, and you can be anyone's Saturn too. It's the situation itself that will create that Saturn dynamic. And it doesn't matter how old you are. Just as parents teach their children, and teachers teach their students, the kids and the students teach the grown-ups just the same. I'm sure you can think of a time in your life when you were young, maybe very young, and the tables turned and your elder learned a lesson from you. These early experiences are your first tastes of what it feels like to be Saturn. And if you like it enough, you will start to seek it out, future CEOs in training that you are!

When someone is schooling you, that's a Saturn moment. When someone is chastising you, that's also a Saturn moment. When someone is telling you what to do, and they are acting like they know better, whether or not they are a confirmed authority on the matter, you are truly in the land of Saturn. Saturn also has a mean side, a cold side, bossy and bitchy, so when your older brother or sister or cousin is telling you to clean your room or to do your homework and they are snide about it and playing parent, they are putting their bad Saturn on you. What do you do? Submit? Fight back?

Anytime you encounter an expert, or a so-called expert, there's the potential for a Saturn encounter. These people claim to know more than you, seek to boss you (and others) around, and can show up as family members, friends, your partner, your ex-wife, your bartender, your landlord, the teller at the bank, random strangers, Internet trolls. They tell you how it is. They tell you what to do and where to go. They take authority like it's nothing to them, easy as rolling out of bed.

Saturn isn't always mean and ugly, though. These Saturn teaching moments can be beautiful.

Your partner or best friend can teach you with kind words and by example. They can model for you the mature responsible way to handle something that's hard for you without making you feel bad in the process. The barista who makes your coffee may have something to teach you as well, and not just about making the perfect foam for a cappuccino. Just like any acquaintance or stranger you meet can give you a hard time, the same random strangers can tell you just what you need to know, right when you need to know it.

I remember visiting an old friend in Ohio who used to be a college professor. I love this friend dearly, and I'm sharing this example because she's such a beautiful Saturn. She has a PhD in Asian religion and is always teaching me and everyone, even though she hasn't taught in the classroom in years. It's just her personality. It's just who she is. Take her to Walmart to shop and she will teach the cashier. Take her out to eat and she's schooling the server. In what, you ask? Does it matter? No matter what topic comes up in conversations, she becomes the teacher all over again, all of a sudden, spotlight on her, holding court.

We all have an example like that from our lives, when such a person gave a helping hand in the form of a lesson and showed us the way out of the dark wood or stopped to tell us how to do something better. This is Saturn stopping time, taking us aside, and giving us a moment we need to learn.

Chapter 4

Saturn in the Signs

There are twelve signs in the zodiac, and your Saturn, like all the planets in your birth chart, will make its home in one of these twelve signs: Aries, Taurus, Gemini, Cancer, Leo, Virgo, Libra, Scorpio, Sagittarius, Capricorn, Aquarius, Pisces.

If you have your Saturn in Aries, for example, then you have your Saturn in Aries always and forever. It won't ever change. We all have our Saturn somewhere, just like we all have our Sun somewhere, and our Moon, and you likely are at least a little familiar with each of the twelve signs, even if you don't know anyone personally who has their Sun in that sign.

The fact that your Saturn makes its home in one of these signs, and not one of the other signs, is part of what makes *you* unique and makes your Saturn different from all the other ones!

Saturn in Taurus will have different life lessons to learn and different gifts to share with the world than Saturn in Cancer or Saturn in Libra. Your Saturn placement has an effect on your personality. It's not just the Sun and Moon and other planets that makes you, *you*. Your Saturn sign matters too. The sign your Saturn is in will affect not only who you are, but also affect the expression of Saturn, whether Saturn can do what it's supposed to!

Let me explain: Every planet in your chart has a job, has a purpose, and Saturn is no exception. One of Saturn's jobs is to help you, literally, do your job, help you finish tasks, help you follow the rules, be disciplined, and not sit around all day watching television and eating cookies (unless that is your job or life purpose!).

Are some Saturn placements more effective than others, better at being Saturn, better at all the good stuff of Saturn and less of the challenging stuff? Absolutely. Saturn symbolizes structure and rules, and some signs are simply better at both.

In this chapter, we will explore the ups and downs of Saturn in each of the twelve signs. Saturn wouldn't be happy if we didn't take a serious and honest look under the hood.

As you read through these Saturn in the signs descriptions, please keep in mind that we must grow into the abilities and talents and best expression and use of our Saturn. It takes time.

In other words, I'm not trying to scare you! Saturn demands we pay attention, follow the rules, and grow up—so that we can become the strong mature humans we are meant to be.

We will exhibit fearful Saturn first in life and exhibit masterful Saturn later in life. There's no skipping steps to maturity, and the older you get, and the more wisdom you acquire, the more you will overcome those fears and limitations of your particular Saturn.

As the years and decades pass, you will begin to show the world all the advantages your Saturn has to offer. You start to give back. The first Saturn Return (see Chapter Six) is the beginning of this maturation process.

You are not only a student of life but also a teacher. There is purpose to your existence. There is a reason why you are here. Saturn definitely holds a key. I know that might sound daunting or hard to believe, but it's the truth. The more you get to know your Saturn, the sign it is in, the house it is in, its interplay with the other items in your chart, the closer you get to discovering that life purpose and the reason why you are here.

Saturn in Aries: The Hero

If your Saturn is in Aries, then you are a natural-born leader, heroic and bold, like a soldier leading a great army—although you may not feel this way at all. And although you will resist the call, you must lead others where they are destined to go. This is your purpose in life, Saturn in Aries. You show us the way.

In your early years, when opportunities arose to lead or shepherd others (and such opportunities did arise) you would likely refuse, terrified of taking charge. This is also part of your path, and the way

Saturn operates in all of our charts, that we must struggle before reaching mastery.

Saturn in Aries is like a world leader or Olympic athlete who isn't sure what to do next. You may gain followers and fans and friends, but due to your lack of faith in yourself, any self-doubt or opposition to your position could cause you to retreat from the metaphorical battlefield. The urge to push through obstacles is met by your fear of the unknown.

Allowing others to rely on you for your innate strength and ability to guide and inspire (which they can see, even if you can't) can make you feel weak, embarrassed, and not up to the task, whatever the task may be.

Despite the intensity of your self-doubt, Saturn in Aries, you have a real gift for knowing exactly what needs to happen first and possibly next. You discover solutions with an envious creative and fiery flair. You are the one who volunteers to drive the getaway car because you are brave and like to drive fast. No hesitation! Your job is to learn decisiveness and positive confident forward movement, like an animal hunting its prey. Do wild animals hesitate? Only when it's part of their overall strategy. You nature is to compete and to win.

But how does one learn decisiveness? You must learn to trust your bold instincts and never look back.

Dear Saturn in Aries, it may take years before you become the leader you are meant to be. Saturn, symbolically, is a slow-moving energy, whereas Aries, associated with the planet Mars, is a fire sign, fast and brave and bright. Saturn is thus likely to slow down Aries's impulsive, impatient, headstrong behavior. You can see how this could be good: Aries may say yes too soon. Aries acts first and thinks later. Saturn in Aries, however, will temper that fire and desire. Saturn in Aries will temper that temper.

Your Gift

Saturn in Aries, your true gift is courage, and yet deep inside you fear standing up for yourself. You may hit too hard like a bullied child on a playground. People already fear you. That's why they bully you. Even when you're shaking, stand tall. This courage is within you. The magic key is to have faith in your instincts. Instincts are your immediate, internal reactions to a situation. Yours are worth trusting. You will sometimes still feel afraid, even as you teach the rest of us how to be brave.

Your Challenge

If you have your Saturn in Aries, then you believe you cannot win no matter what you do. You believe you cannot assert yourself for fear of reprisal or losing.

Throughout your life, you will find yourself in situations where you are being asked to take charge, and your life lessons and self-development depend on what you choose. Not every battle is worth fighting. Do you jump? Do you take a breath and wait and evaluate? You must find the balance between patience and trusting your impulses.

Saturn in Aries can be terrified of being alone and look to others for approval, but Aries and Mars rule independence and the pioneering spirit and separation. Aries is a hunter. When Saturn is in Aries, you must balance these two sides, caution and force.

Your Ambition

You long to rule. You long to be in charge. You long to make decisions without backtracking or fence-sitting. You long for certainty in an uncertain world. You long to trust yourself and to move forward in your life with bravery.

Do take risks.

Do pick your battles.

Do lead with fairness.

Don't hide.

Don't avoid.

Don't shy away from a challenge.

If you have a Saturn in Aries person in your life, then you want to encourage their independence and decision-making ability.

Give the Saturn in Aries child the opportunity to initiate action. For example, let your child choose whether to color or to play with dolls or to reach out to a friend for a play date rather than you, the caretaker, making that decision. You want to encourage their self-confidence.

Give the Saturn in Aries employee the opportunity to lead a meeting or teleconference. They may try to defer to you or find a partner to collaborate with. Your job is to let them know that they can handle it.

Give your Saturn in Aries friend time alone. Saturn in Aries needs space but may not feel comfortable taking it. Saturn in Aries looks for validation from others. You can give it by being there when they need you but without spending every waking moment texting back and forth.

Give your Saturn in Aries spouse or partner the message that they can trust their instincts and follow their passions. They already err on the side of caution and fear. It's perfectly fine to remind them that they don't need anyone's approval to *live*.

If you have a Saturn in Aries person in your life, then you will have to learn to stand back and be quiet, leave room for him to take the reigns and figure out how to run his own life, and that it is safe to do so.

Your job, whether as parent or boss or friend or spouse or teacher or life coach, is to provide an opportunity or guideline for them and then get out of the way so that they can choose what to do first.

Saturn in Aries must learn to make wise creative decisions from the head and heart.

Saturn in Taurus: The Beauty

When your Saturn is in Taurus, you fear rejection. You fear rejection based on your appearance, what others think of your clothes, your face. You suspect that your "outside" will never be good enough, that somehow you always fall short.

Remember that Taurus is ruled by Venus, and Venus rules the beautiful. With Saturn in Taurus, you feel there's a limit to how pretty or handsome or valuable you are.

You also fear rejection based on what you own, your material possessions, your money, your social class, your taste. You may even literally fear being seen and refuse to make eye contact. Some Saturn in Taurus will become reclusive.

The irony, however, is that you likely have an extraordinary, unique beauty and artistic talent, especially when you spend the effort *and* money.

"Spend" is the key word here. Spend the time. Spend the money. The difference in how you look and how you feel will change your life.

Remember that Saturn rules *effort,* and Saturn will make it hard for Saturn in Taurus to express what comes naturally to Taurus, like comfort in nature or putting dogged effort into skin care. For Saturn in Taurus, attention to looking good is not shallow behavior. Rather, it's an indicator of wisdom.

Taurus men and women the world over are known for their lovely appearance, refusal to be rushed, and ability to enjoy the pleasures of life, like good food and wine, sunny vacations and relaxation. Your Saturn in Taurus will make you shy away from such things and feel you don't deserve them, avoid them, or find them scary. You consider the world of Taurus *not for you.* No beauty, no money, no love.

Taurus is stubborn and immoveable once the mind is made up. With Saturn in Taurus you will not learn your life lessons until you bust through the Saturn walls as often and as strongly as you avoid and refuse.

Dear Saturn in Taurus, I know you feel unable to attract or seduce what you need to survive. Do not eschew beauty and surface appearances. Learn to enhance what you have.

Your Gift

Your gift is that you are a person of substance. You are spiritually rich. If you have your Saturn in Taurus, you place less emphasis on money and things and status, and instead you value the inner qualities of a person. You do not judge a book by its cover or prefer a rich man or woman over a poor one. You may even be an ascetic, feeling like you need own nothing, just a place to lay your head and a book to read. You know that no dollar bill accompanies the grave.

Because of these qualities, many seek to be your friend and to learn from you this more spiritual perspective. They find you refreshing because you do not seek to compete with others, and you show them another way to live and be. They believe you have something they don't and it's true! You have peace of mind because you know everything material will fade.

Your gift is your ability to see deeply into others. You look past all appearances and glimpse people as they truly are, in their soul naked glory.

Your Challenge

One of your challenges is to make money and be financially stable. You must learn to live in *this* world and not abandon it, to not avoid the material world altogether. Because Saturn in Taurus values the inside so much, he or she can neglect the outside, which can lead to living from paycheck to paycheck and never saving a dime. Since one of your life lessons is to *spend money,* like a good Taurus, you have to figure out how to earn the money!

Every Saturn in Taurus should learn to garden, nurture plant life for food or beauty or both. I see you with a beautiful rose garden, Saturn in Taurus. This garden is a metaphor for the moneymaking process or perhaps the moneymaking is a metaphor for the garden. Both the garden and the money are symbolic. The reality is that Saturn in Taurus must learn abundance, learn how to make bank accounts and gardens and self-esteem grow.

Your Ambition

You long to feel beautiful and comfortable in your skin. You long to look in the mirror and not hate what you see. You long to have nice things despite your fears and mistrust of the physical world. You long to not worry where the next dollar is coming from.

Do beautify your body.

Do spend money on yourself.

Do seek serenity.

Don't ignore your home décor.

Don't let your bank account get to zero.

Don't starve yourself.

If you have a Saturn in Taurus person in your life, you can show him how to attract what he wants and needs.

Give your Saturn in Taurus child lots of praise. The Saturn in Taurus child needs to know that her face and body and appearance overall is perfect just the way it is and as good as the other kids'. Saturn in Taurus insecurity is particularly rooted in physical inferiority. Fear not that too much praise will create a big ego. Saturn in our charts shows a deficiency in self-esteem and self-belief, across all the signs, so please go above and beyond in teaching self-esteem to your child. *Do* tell your Saturn in Taurus daughter that she's pretty.

Give the Saturn in Taurus employee tasks that require diligence and making things grow. Saturn in Taurus will inhibit that famous Taurus inclination for patience and slowness. Saturn in Taurus people tend to be nervous. Do not rush them. Their best work happens when they can pause even in the midst of a project.

Give the Saturn in Taurus friend lots of hugs (definitely ask first!). Saturn in Taurus feels uncomfortable in his body, and a friend's hugs can be healing and help him feel safe. Remember that Taurus is an earth sign, rooted, but Saturn in Taurus is afraid to be stable. When a friend is in crisis, touch her hand, touch her shoulder.

Tell your Saturn in Taurus partner or spouse how attracted you are, how sexy they are, how good looking. Don't put a cap on your loving words or gestures. Of course, this will make them feel squeamish at first, but deep healing can result. Taurus is known for being possessive, perhaps the most possessive of the zodiac. Saturn in Taurus will feel self-conscious about this characteristic, so let them know you accept! You belong to them!

If you have a Saturn in Taurus person in your life, remind her that she is beautiful and delightful, body and soul, without caveat or exception. Let him know that it's okay to be here, on the earth, in a body—not only to survive, but to thrive.

Saturn in Gemini:
The Writer

Gemini rules words, so when your Saturn is in Gemini, you can literally be afraid to speak, afraid to write, to use your voice, to share your thoughts and perceptions.

You may even be afraid to show the real you to your family and friends. You may express the opinions of others as though they were your own. Those closest to you may wonder who the real you really is! Remember that Saturn, first and foremost, is our fear. Saturn in Gemini will stutter, literally or metaphorically.

Some of you Saturn in Gemini will even pretend to be less smart than you are, and you are super smart! You will have trouble finding the right word, and that will make you nervous. Prone to overthinking and panic attacks, you feel it is safer to play dumb.

Others may accuse you of the "silent treatment" when you feel like being quiet. The truth is that sometimes you just need a break from thinking. Thinking can make you tired, and even if you are an extrovert, being too social can drain you.

Especially in the younger years, the Saturn in Gemini person will have trouble expressing precisely what they mean and what they need. You require patient parents who will give you the space to find the right word. That phrase "use your words" was invented for Saturn in Gemini.

As a child you may have been excessively quiet or introverted or refused to speak, and maybe you did have a stutter. As a grown-up in the world, however, you will learn to share your ideas with confidence and even pleasure. The ideal mature Saturn in Gemini loves words and loves to be clever and is happy to talk and flirt. She doesn't fear witty repartee.

Dear Saturn in Gemini, like all the Saturn placements, you must move from struggle and fear to mastery. Once you reach this level, you will become the published author, speaker of many languages, journalist, novelist, creator of crossword puzzles, speech writer, public speaker, fearless in sharing your point of view.

Gemini is a successful dealmaker in part because he can speak persuasively, but the Saturn in Gemini struggle is word for word.

Your Gift

Professor or poet, you have a way with words unlike any other. You have a gift for finding the best word, the most accurate word, no matter the circumstance. Gemini is the writer and communicator of the zodiac, and Saturn, of course, will slow down your facility, put the brakes on, fill you with hesitation. Saturn will make you doubt and pause because that's what Saturn does, what Saturn is supposed to do.

Despite your fears, however, you are brilliant and eloquent and instinctively know when to speak and when to be quiet.

Saturn will not make you a plodding or dull writer or speechmaker. Instead, Saturn makes you both editor and writer in one, crossing out all the unnecessary words even before they leave your head. Just make sure Saturn doesn't cross out the whole book!

Your Challenge

Your challenge is to sit down and do it. Sit down at the desk and not get up. To master words and language and sharing your thoughts with the world, while battling your lack of confidence, you have to sequester yourself and get to work. It can be lonely. You must learn to multitask without falling apart. You must include writing practice in your daily life.

You will resist going with the Gemini flow. You will resist the waves and spurts of Gemini language joy. You may feel your clever witticisms aren't substantial enough, but you must jump into the sea of words and swim. Don't overedit before you even have a chance to set pen to paper or finger to keyboard.

Become a human dictionary. That's the goal here. Become comfortable with the pages and pages of words and word origins, knowing that you can always shut the book when you reach your limit. Saturn protects us all, but for you to fulfill your destiny, you must bargain with Saturn, let the old man know you got this. Write him a letter. Talk to him personally.

Your Ambition

You long to not feel overwhelmed by your own thoughts. You long to unstrap your focus and multi-task. You long to fluidly write and speak your mind. You long to interact with friends without awkwardness or social anxiety.

Do send letters.

Do write a book.

Do two or more things at once.

Don't clam up.

Don't hide your true thoughts.

Don't skip school.

If you have a Saturn in Gemini person in your life, encourage them to track down the right words for their thoughts and feelings.

Give the Saturn in Gemini child plenty of books to read and games to play and lots of mental stimulation. Word games! Building toys! Gemini rules the hands. Give your child a dictionary and a thesaurus. Read to them. Teach them to read.

Give the Saturn in Gemini employee more than one thing to do. Saturn in Gemini must learn to multitask without stress and handle more than one project at a time. People often criticize Gemini for being scattered, but Saturn in Gemini will fear letting the mind wander. Have them edit or write the employee handbook.

Give your Saturn in Gemini friend a moment to get their thoughts together. Don't push or rush them to talk. Don't talk when they're talking. Saturn will slow down Gemini's natural fluency, quickness, and impulse to chatter. Let them take their time and meander.

Give your Saturn in Gemini spouse or partner a day at the library with you. Gemini rules short trips! Walk around the library, up and down the aisles, looking at the books, touching their spines, selecting. Then you can read to teach other, gently, side by side, whispering. Fill your Saturn in Gemini love with words. Poetry refrigerator magnets would make an excellent gift!

If you have a Saturn in Gemini person in your life, know that there is a writer, a *real* writer, inside of them, aching to come out, and they probably will not rest until they've met it. Encourage them to journal or blog and to discover the best medium for them. Remind them that they can make peace between themselves and their mind through the written word.

Saturn in Cancer:
The Mother

Cancer is the mother of the zodiac, nurturing, creative, intuitive. She gives life.

When your Saturn is in Cancer, your nurturing style, how you take care of yourself or others, will be more fatherly, more Saturnian than motherly Cancerian.

Saturn puts a dam over Cancer's watery flow, and the moon maiden goes into hiding. Cancer is always feeling something, but Saturn says, not right now. Although blessed with creativity and intuition, Saturn in Cancer will have difficulty expressing other typical Cancer traits such as vulnerability, attachment, and emotional openness. No heart on sleeve here!

Saturn in Cancer may even shut her- or himself off from people and relationships out of anxiety because Saturn in Cancer dare not face her or his own deep emotional needs. It's so much easier not to face them.

Another scenario is the Saturn in Cancer who will attach to those who cannot possibly return the love and bonding they crave. This allows Saturn in Cancer to stay stuck and safe, and safety is yet another thing that Cancer must have.

There is only so far you can go with Saturn in Cancer before the emotions turn off and you reach the wall of Saturn. Both giving love and receiving love are affected. It's like the thermostat on a water tank. Once you set the dial, the water can get no hotter, unless an adjustment is made.

Dear Saturn in Cancer, you don't have to change for anyone. We love you just the way you are, *but* if you feel emotionally cut off or that you don't have the love and warmth you hunger for, then you will have to do the inner work. And to complicate matters even further, Saturn in Cancer describes not only the way you nurture self and others but also the kind of nurturing you received as a child. The wound goes way back.

Your Gift

Your gift is inner strength. You're a tough cookie. Even when you feel like you're falling apart, you really are a dependable rock.

You are the one they come to for practical assurance and honest assessment. No sugarcoating. You tell the truth even when the truth might hurt. Your confidants don't mind your sharp style because it comes from a place of integrity. You love with limits, and that makes your loved ones feel safe.

Saturn in Cancer, you are also a fierce and protective parent. If anyone dare try to harm your child (biological or not), then they will have to go through you first. You would tear them apart with your teeth.

Similarly, if someone dares to hurt your own feelings, then there may be no coming back. The door to your heart shuts and Saturn won't permit a reentry. That's when the famous Cancerian sensitivity comes to life. I consider this a gift because you know who is good for you and who isn't. You have boundaries.

Your Challenge

Saturn in Cancer must learn to soften and nurture herself in this lifetime. Nurturing others is secondary to that goal but will follow. You must care for yourself the way you wish your mother had. Saturn in Cancer people often had neglectful or abusive caretakers who did not show them consistent dependable love.

Saturn doesn't want Cancer's tears and memory lanes and nostalgia and becomes impatient with these emotional displays, finding them pointless. Because of this, you can seem cold to others, even though on the inside you wish you could feel what they feel, and in fact you do.

Your challenge is to accept that you have all kinds of feelings and that it's okay to have them and it's okay to cry. Your challenge is to let your soft and silly side out to play. Cancers are silly!

Your Ambition

Saturn in Cancer, your ambitions are so primal and personal. You long to be loved. You long to love. You long to be mothered. You long to mother. I also believe your ambition is not to need anyone at all, ever, but you will not grow and reach your potential if you follow only the discipline of Saturn and ignore the caring of Cancer.

Do heal your inner child.

Do learn about self-love.

Do nurture others.

Don't punish yourself.

Don't punish others.

Don't be alone.

If you have a Saturn in Cancer person in your life, please love him as though he were your own child.

Give your Saturn in Cancer child plenty of opportunities to attach and bond with you. They may not feel your love, through no fault of your own, and you will have to find what works. Discover your child's love language and learn to speak it. Maybe they need to hear "I love you" more than touch or vice versa. Cuddles are recommended. Visit the beach! Sand and sea will soothe your child.

Give your Saturn in Cancer employee assignments they will feel emotionally connected to, projects they can mother. Find out what those might be. Even better if they can birth a project and watch it grow. You will get your best job performance from Saturn in Cancer when the office environment feels like a family and they get to be matriarch or patriarch.

Give your Saturn in Cancer friend plenty of space. Do not hover. Do not expect your Saturn in Cancer friend to take care of you like a Cancer Sun or Moon would, with lots of fussing and homemade chicken soup (although they may be a fabulous cook). Respect their solitude. They find their peace of mind when alone.

Give your Saturn in Cancer spouse or partner not only the solitude they crave (as with the Saturn in Cancer friend) but also lots of tenderness and soothing. Cook for them. Your Saturn in Cancer love may resist your approach at first, but the path to healing Saturn's harshness is not to starve the body and soul of love but to feed it, a little at a time—bite size, if need be. Hugs, kisses, gentleness, caring, mothering. You can even set aside times to practice hugging or practice nurturing. Saturn in Cancer needs love to have structure. Saturn = practice. Cancer = protection.

If you have a Saturn in Cancer person in your life, teach them that tears are good and cleansing medicine. Show them that sensitivity and vulnerability are strengths, not weaknesses. Tell them that they can heal their inner child pain simply by letting emotions flow and that you will be there for them, no matter their mood. Accept all their moods, especially the ones they don't!

Saturn in Cancer truly wants to be a vessel of love, but isn't always sure how. The more love and acceptance you show them, the more safe they will feel to feel.

Saturn in Leo: The Star

When your Saturn is in Leo, you will shun the spotlight—even though you may ache to be a star of stage or screen, even though you hunger for attention, adoration, to see your name in lights. No matter your profession, when your Saturn is in Leo, you *resist* the call.

Your purpose in life is to get over it! Your purpose in life is to release any self-doubt about your charisma, talent, and star power. Your craving may be for fame and fortune or simply to be recognized in your field of expertise. A great actor with talent to spare and connections galore with Saturn in Leo will self-sabotage and get in their own way. They may stay with an agent or manager that they *know* cannot get them the roles that will catapult them out of obscurity and onto the Hollywood walk of fame.

Saturn in Leo can be shy or timid about their gifts, and this doesn't apply to only performers. Remember that Leo is ruled by the Sun and the Sun is who we are. The Sun is our ego, identity, essence. Saturn in Leo will make you feel small and put the brakes on who and what you think you can become. It's not only about hiding from the spotlight but also hiding from who you truly are.

You may have dreams of being a pilot, but Saturn, which rules ambition, and Leo, which rules your self, will convince you that your dream is pointless or totally out of reach. Leo *must* shine, and Saturn in Leo must make peace with this. Leo must toss their hair, smile, and call attention to itself. A healthy Leo has a healthy ego, but Saturn in Leo is a sad lion. The ego has been robbed of its natural luster.

Your purpose in life, dear Saturn in Leo, is not to hide in the shadows but to be seen and known and praised for your gifts! That phrase "don't hide your light under a bushel" could have been written about you.

Your Gift

Your gift is your generosity. You give others room to breathe. You let them be who they are.

For example, you won't make a conversation with a friend all about you. Instead, you'll share the spotlight and not try to keep it all for yourself. This makes you very popular among your friends because they know that they can share their good news with you and you will be genuinely happy for them. You believe everyone deserves a chance to be seen and known and to shine. Even if you did most of the job yourself, you will give others credit because you know you couldn't have done it alone.

Saturn in Leo, you see the value in group effort, in everybody putting their heads together to solve a problem. You don't believe anyone is better or more special than anyone else. You are fair and wise and humble.

Your Challenge

Your challenge is to stop being so damn humble and to grab a little stardom for yourself. Your challenge is to see yourself as special and deserving of accolades for a job well done or just because you exist! You deserve to be here too. You are unique too.

Saturn in Leo, you must also strive to be the *best* at something, compete to get there, and then be admired for your artistry and prowess. You will succeed if you put in the effort.

Your job is to seek glory, recognition, prizes, but not only that. You must also learn to see that glory and prizes just for *you,* only for you, without the obligation to share with anyone, is okay. No guilt for standing apart from the crowd.

You have such a deep humility, Saturn in Leo, that you will find it tacky to toot your own horn, but toot you must. Your low self-esteem, your Sun, needs some shoulders to stand on so that you can touch the stars.

Your Ambition

You long for the courage to be yourself. You long for the courage to be seen. You long to perform, sing, dance, act, write, paint, build, create, *play!* You long to be proud of who you are. You long for a life as beautiful and everlasting as the sun.

Do stand out.

Do share your gifts.

Do toot your own horn!

Don't hide your face.

Don't refuse to shine.

Don't deny your dreams.

If you have a Saturn in Leo person in your life, encourage them to be themselves and to share that special self with the whole world.

Give the Saturn in Leo child plenty of games and toys to inspire their creativity like coloring books, sidewalk chalk, stories about artists. Let them cook with you and make up recipes. Tell them it's okay to color outside the lines.

Leos are naturally creative and natural leaders, but Saturn in Leo will be fearful and sometimes come on too strong. Show your Saturn in Leo child how to relax and play and have fun. The playground isn't a battleground where they need to be the boss.

Let your child discover what they love. Let your child discover their own sense of fun and play.

Give the Saturn in Leo employee tasks that require them to stand out and take charge. Don't let them hide in group projects, letting others take credit for their hard work. Saturn in Leo is all about the *team,* but the truth is that Saturn in Leo stands out from the team. They need to get used to being recognized for their unique contributions because many Saturn in Leo will someday be the boss. Nurture this! Putting their name on a project would be a nice touch. It may scare them and yet secretly thrill them and push them toward new creative heights.

Give the Saturn in Leo friend a night out at karaoke, even if they resist. Encourage them to sing loud and proud. Take an improv class together. Go see plays together. Leo rules the theatre and loves to have fun and play, but Saturn in Leo may be too serious for their own health. You can help them loosen up. Buy them a crown or tiara!

Give your Saturn in Leo partner or spouse lots of romance, compliments, and your undivided attention. Your Saturn in Leo partner or spouse will say: I'm not worthy! But I recommend you continue. Saturn is a hard part in all of our charts. It shows our suffering. But the more love and fun and play you bring to your relationship, the more they will relax and purr. Remind them how magnificent they are. Remind them that it's never too late to have a happy childhood. They can have it with you!

When you have a Saturn in Leo person in your life, your job is to cheer them on without hesitation. Love them! Be proud of them! Let them know how you feel! Leo is supposed to be confident, but when Saturn is in Leo, it takes a big bite out of this normal and typical Leo trait. With your help and love, they can become the king or queen they need to be.

Saturn in Virgo: The Help

Dear Saturn in Virgo, you need order in your life, folders and color-coded Post-its! You need alphabetization and lists that stay neat forever. Clutter is your enemy.

Dear Saturn in Virgo, your sheets should stay clean, your kitchen floor spotless, your filing system beyond compare. Know where everything is at all times. Everything in its place. Perfection is what you must be striving for along with grammatically correct sentences. And worry. Don't forget to worry.

You'll never get there of course—none of us will—but it's the trying, the effort, that counts!

Many Virgos excel at all of the above, but when Saturn is in Virgo, these natural Virgo skills and affinities take a hard hit. You may resist organization or order or just be bad at it. If you have other Virgo placements in your chart, you might be neat and clear with some things and then in a dream world with others. See, with Saturn it's not actually all or nothing. You may have some mastery here, but immaturity there.

Remember that Saturn instills fear and self-doubt in us, so you may fear that you or it, the task at hand, will never be good enough, perfect enough, and thus you don't even try. You let things fall apart.

Saturn in Virgo, however, must master the following Virgo skills among others: note-taking;

list-making; proper use of the comma; the clean or at least organized desk, kitchen, and house; details; seeing the trees, not the forest; caring for small animals; being responsible and ethical with your work, no cutting corners, doing a good job. Humility. It's a lot, right? Well, that's Virgo for you. The work never ends.

Mercury is the ruler of Virgo, and in Virgo, Mercury's job may also be the writer; but Virgo is more about perfection and precision of routines, health, habits, nutrition, the body, and purity and excellence of mind. Clear thinking. Analysis. Virgo is *good,* but Saturn in Virgo doesn't want to be good. Saturn in Virgo thinks *good* isn't good enough.

Your job is to make your body and habits and routines and daily life an organized and smoothly running machine. Efficient and effective. Pay attention to the small things, to every detail.

If your Saturn is in Virgo, though, you are going to refuse or resist this call to order and forget to pay bills or take your vitamins or even know what a vitamin is. You buy them and let them waste away in the cupboard. You get sick because you refuse to really *be* in your body, and this is very un-Virgo of you, which is what Saturn does when it's in a sign.

What you fail to understand: things *can* be improved even if not made perfect.

Your Gift

Saturn in Virgo, your gift is compassion. You give people the benefit of the doubt. You see them with a good eye. You trust them. When friends or family are in trouble, they know they can lean on you. You listen to them, fuss over them, and then end the evening with some spiritual yet practical advice. You see the big picture. You know just what to say to put worried hearts and minds at ease.

You have a generous, expansive spirit, and whatever you have, you give, be it money, shelter, guidance, gifts, maybe even the shirt off your back. You do not judge the needs or requests of others because you know how it feels to be judged. When you dole out your famous advice, it's like you can see someone's entire life before your eyes and what they need to do to get back on track. Some would even say you have the gift of second sight.

Even when you're under the weather or too busy to breathe, out-of-town guests are more than welcome in your home. Your hospitality goes above and beyond.

Your Challenge

Saturn in Virgo, you must learn boundaries around your body, your time, your energy. You must learn that even if you believe in reincarnation or that the soul is eternal, your physical body is a finite thing and needs your time and attention and care.

You have a tendency to get run down. Why? Because you can't help but give too much, do too much, offer too much. You don't know where you end and everyone else begins. What's mine is theirs, you say, but it's making you sick, my dear.

Another hardy challenge is your steadfast desire to *not* be present. "Be here now" is not your motto. Being here now is unthinkable when it's so much easier and more fun to escape.

The "ideal" Virgo Sun or Moon is pretty comfortable with reality and the present moment, but with Saturn in Virgo, you seek the way out through television, food, sex, drinking, *work*.

Your challenge is to examine the details of your life, your habits and routines, and evaluate how well they serve you. Are you functional or dysfunctional? Somewhere in between?

Your Ambition

You long to put your life in order. You long to have a clean house. You long to help people even more than you already do. You long to not have a body or bodily functions and instead to float above the world, no stress! You long to ditch the daily grind. You long to disappear. You long to do nothing wrong, ever.

Do have a job.

Do get that mysterious ache checked out.

Do have a schedule.

Don't overindulge in drugs or drink.

Don't be late.

Don't diss the details.

If you have a Saturn in Virgo person in your life, help them organize their life. Remind them it doesn't have to be perfect.

Give your Saturn in Virgo child opportunities to sort and select and organize. The Saturn in Virgo child should be enlisted in housework duty: folding clothes, putting groceries away, returning toys back to the toy chest, cleaning his or her own room are just a few examples. Virgo is normally and naturally diligent, but the Saturn in Virgo child may prefer to diligently daydream only. Ask them their opinion. Ask for their advice. Virgo loves to help and be of service to others, but Saturn in Virgo may feel their ideas aren't good enough.

Give your Saturn in Virgo employee small jobs, and by small, I mean detailed. They need to learn to work precisely and efficiently and see the trees, not just the forest or big picture of a project. Your Saturn in Virgo employee may rush to finish when really they need to slow down and retrace their steps. Give them time to edit but with firm deadlines. Give them privacy to focus and concentrate.

Give your Saturn in Virgo friend a helping hand. Saturn in Virgo is a disorganized collector, and they need you to help them dig out of the chaos. Have regular hang-out time with your friend. Establish regular routines. Share with them your favorite health podcasts or techniques for getting unstuck. Of course, if you also have Saturn in Virgo, then you may just fuel each other's chaos!

Give your Saturn in Virgo spouse or partner the very clear message that it's okay to say no.

Sure, you can remind them to go to the doctor and be their human alarm clock and all the other quotidian Virgo-type things, but the most important deed you can do for your Saturn in Virgo true love is to encourage their backbone. Saturn in Virgo will give to depletion. Their bountiful spirit is partly why you fell in love with them. Let them know it's perfectly fine to pick and choose who to trust, love, spend time with. Reassure them that making judgments won't make them a bad person but instead makes them a *smart* person.

If you have a Saturn in Virgo person in your life, then you have met chaos. You know them by name! Your job is to show them that putting their life in order won't take away from its wonder or fun or fantasy. On the contrary, learning Virgo ways will lower their stress and raise their self-confidence.

Saturn in Libra: The Lover

Libra loves love. Libra is supposed to love love. But if your Saturn is in Libra? You may be terrified of love, especially committed love, especially marriage.

In the zodiac, Libra rules committed relation-ships and partnerships, personal and business. Libra also rules ideas such as balance, fairness, and justice. Libra Suns and Moons and Ascendants are the *we*-people, not the *me*-people, of the zodiac. They prefer to include others and don't like to think, or be, alone.

Saturn in Libra, however, may go it *alone* and be perfectly fine, thank you very much! Or they partner with someone whom they don't really like or love. Saturn in Libra doesn't realize that they do this. Similar to all the Saturn placements, it helps to have others point out what we cannot see for ourselves.

Some Saturn in Libra people will avoid marriage or other partnerships, and the responsibilities of partnerships, until much later in life. In order to learn the lessons of Saturn, though, you have to keep dealing with people until you get it right. You can't hide away on a mountaintop somewhere, living a life of solitude and actually *grow* the way Saturn wants you to. Saturn wants your engagement.

You, Saturn in Libra, must get into the nitty-gritty details of people's lives, be concerned with other people genuinely, not in a fake or surface way. You find yourself by finding others and not the other way around. You would make a great marriage counselor for this reason. You can observe and learn for years before trying it yourself!

Saturn in Libra's job is thus to gain mastery over the realm of relationship, partnership, alliance, truce, commitment to others. You must deal with other people, closely, one-on-one, and not be afraid. You have to learn to give and take. Learn fairness and balance with another person. Take turns!

Young Saturn in Libra is like the most boisterous Aries, thinking only of themselves, but the mature Saturn in Libra realizes that they cannot make it alone in this life and that life is more beautiful when they put effort into building alliances and getting along with others. Life continually comes to a full Saturn stop when Saturn in Libra tries to do everything herself. Saturn in Libra, you *need* other people. And they need you. Once you realize this, life clicks into place.

Libra is ruled by Venus (like Taurus), but Libra is an air sign, so Saturn in Libra may err on the side of emotion and refuse to use their wise mind and logic to solve their relationship problems. They will refuse to see both sides of an issue or be unable to see both sides. They will act too fast, too impulsively.

Libra tends to deliberate. We accuse them of fence-sitting, but when Saturn is in Libra, they rush in and do what they feel is best no matter what anyone else thinks. Saturn in Libra must learn to slow down, learn tact, ask for others' feedback. Trying to understand the needs of others will make your life run smoothly. Saturn in Libra's motto should be "Life is with people."

Your Gift

Your gift is your independence of spirit. You don't require anyone else's permission to live. People look up to you because they want to be like you. You're a leader. You know who you are. People see you doing your thing and not caring what others think.

Let them judge! You will still do what you want anyway! You're passionate! Your passion feeds you and others. Your take-charge attitude wins you admirers. You're popular and you teach others that they too can live by their own rules.

Saturn in Libra, you don't wait. You don't spend forever hemming and hawing about what to do next or take decades to plot your next move. This is

intuitive, creative behavior and it works for you—
up to a point.

Your Challenge

Your challenge is that you are scared to death
of other people, and this can make you seem closed
off or critical of others. You do what you please, yes,
but in your heart you fear rejection. What if they
don't approve of you? What if they don't like you?
You act like you don't care, but this isn't the whole
truth. You do care. You care a lot.

Saturn in Libra, you must learn to live in the
world. You must learn to be social and learn at least
some social graces so that you feel more comfortable
in your interactions with others. Saturn wants you
to be less clumsy and to live in harmony amongst
the other humans. Remember that Saturn requires
our work! Effort! It's not always painless.

It's hard for you to see both sides, Saturn in
Libra. It's hard for you to take your time. It's hard
for you to care what others think. It's hard for you
to prioritize beauty and grace, and yet Saturn
won't let you off the hook until you change, even
just a little.

Learning to walk in high heels with a book on your head would be good training for Saturn in Libra. Why? Grace under pressure.

Your Ambition

You long to be beautiful and kind. You long to be part of a couple. You long to be less lonely. You long to truly understand the needs of others. You long to be an artist, to create beautiful works of art. You long to learn compromise without sacrificing your fierceness!

Do make art.

Do tend to your appearance.

Do cultivate relationships of all kinds.

Don't be a lone wolf.

Don't burn bridges.

Don't run away.

If you have a Saturn in Libra person in your life, your job is to include them! Don't leave them out. Show them how you make others feel cared about. Encourage cooperation. Saturn in Libra will shy away from others, but Saturn in Libra needs to live, work, be, create with others.

Give the Saturn in Libra child time with other children. Schedule play dates! Make sure they have friends and aren't loners. Help them play nicely. Take note if they bully or feel bullied. When problems with friends or authority figures arise, are they able to understand the other person's point of view?

Practice decision-making skills with your child. Help them think things through. What would they rather have for dinner? Don't just pick the simplest thing to make or the most tasty. What other factors should we consider? The time it takes? The ingredients we have on hand? The two of you should agree! Teach them how to share.

Give the Saturn in Libra employee plenty of opportunity to work beside others, even if they feel uncomfortable. Don't let them run roughshod or play boss. On the outside, they may appear to be team players and talk a good talk, but the truth is, they need help with this mindset.

The Saturn in Libra employee wants to go it alone, whether or not they care about taking credit for a job well done or ultimate outcomes. Why bother with compromise and cooperation when it's easier to do it myself, Saturn in Libra thinks. I don't need anyone, Saturn in Libra thinks. In reality, however, as their boss or supervisor, you can teach them workplace skills that will last them a lifetime: how to get along with others.

Give harmony to your Saturn in Libra friend. Go to the symphony together or other music and art events. Take a painting or photography class with them. Museum trips. Fashion shows! Discover fine arts and crafts and symmetry together. Help them with their look. Tell them what colors and styles are the most flattering. Your Saturn in Libra friend needs more approval from others than they let on!

Give your Saturn in Libra spouse or partner your word. You committed to them, so make sure you walk the walk and not just talk the talk. Saturn in Libra fears having to fend for him- or herself so be consistently loving, loyal, supportive.

Don't go to sleep mad. When you fight, make sure to reach a compromise as soon as possible. Make decisions together. Live together! Cooperate and collaborate.

Work on your relationship. Seek guidance from others. Go on marriage or relationship retreats.

Study together how to be better partners. Study love. Study commitment. Put effort into making each other happy. Make sure the division of labor in the home and in the relationship is fair, balanced, and equal.

When you have a Saturn in Libra person in your life, your job is to show them that relationships are good and safe places to be, that it's okay to rely on others and commit to them and share responsibilities. Saturn in Libra, you will not lose yourself by caring for others, and the more you care, the more others will see you and want to be with you.

Saturn in Libra, you don't have to be lonely. Reach out.

Saturn in Scorpio:
The Alchemist

Scorpio goes to extremes. Scorpio obsesses. They love with passion and they hate with passion. You will rarely find a Scorpio without an opinion. They take sides. Scorpio isn't afraid to dive deep into topics that many prefer to avoid, like death, sex, money, the supernatural. They tend to be secretive, though, so you may not know their latest obsession. *Saturn* in Scorpio, however, will resist all of this and more.

When I talk about sex in regards to Scorpio, I don't mean the perfect world of the Photoshopped men and women that we see in advertising. Scorpio sex has a special keyword: intimacy. *Really* getting to know someone. Penetrating their spirit. For Scorpio, sex and death are not mere physical acts. They are transformative experiences, and one's soul is intimately involved in both.

Saturn in Scorpio, though, will fear this intimate journey, fear that the depths of human emotion and intensity will swallow them whole. They would rather stay safe in the simple, physical, material world of money and possessions and surface beauty. The drive to explore the deep, the dark, the private, the intimate, the frightening, the truly taboo is dramatically reduced or repressed.

When your Saturn is in Scorpio, you may think you are a fearless badass, willing to confront the forbidden. But when faced with it, you run, preferring an easier, more relaxing experience of life, instead of all these people with their messy, nasty emotions and motivations. You're a detective afraid to detect. You fear change, and you fear death.

And yet, Saturn in Scorpio is one of the most powerful Saturns. Once you master the lessons inherent in your sign, you become a healer of souls. You're the psychoanalyst who perceives others' flaws and fears and feelings, especially the ugly ones we're ashamed of, but doesn't judge. We all need such a person in our lives!

Saturn in Scorpio will *try* to live on the surface, indulging in the material and ignoring the spiritual, but the more they do this and avoid their deeper self and the deeper selves of others, the more unfulfilled they will feel.

For Saturn in Scorpio to learn their lessons, they have to get their hands and hearts dirty. Remember that Saturn requires that we learn how to *do* the sign it's in (in our individual charts). It's a call to action.

Ideally, self-exploration and self-inquiry will lead to self-acceptance, and then Saturn in Scorpio becomes the best friend you've ever had, the one who sees you at your worst and doesn't look away but supports you, embraces you.

Your Gift

Saturn in Scorpio, you have the gift of clear seeing, clairvoyance. You see deep into our hearts. You know who we are. This can manifest for you as literal psychic ability, knowing what's going to happen before it happens—but you're also excellent at knowing why people do what they do. You understand human behavior and motivation better than anyone, and this can scare us. It can scare you too! Clarity isn't always pretty or nice or comfortable.

Some Saturn in Scorpio may even become professional psychics despite being skeptical, claiming that psychic skill is merely the ability to figure people out. Nevertheless, Saturn in Scorpio can tell you tell you where you lost your keys.

Once you decide it's safe to commit, you're loyal for life and you support people during their darkest hours, emotionally, financially, spiritually. And because you can go deep with people, once you lose the fear side of Saturn, you help them transform, you help them heal their pain. Under your care, wounds becomes wells of healing waters. You're a healer, transformer, alchemist.

Your Challenge

You are terrified of your own darker impulses and those of others, but this is fundamentally what you must explore. This fear, which is Saturn's influence, is actually a green light, not a red light, although of course it doesn't feel that way. You must dive in.

Sure, on the surface you may be interested in any number of taboo topics, such as witchcraft or true crime or trauma, mental illness, but when you get close to it, you can't breathe.

Your challenge is to face yourself first, rather than aiming your laser-beam penetrating insight onto your friends' quirks. You must first reckon with the parts of your psyche and personality that you find intolerable or repulsive, and then through therapy and self-growth, learn to accept your whole self. All of it! Only then do you become a catalyst for others and show them the way through the dark.

Dear Saturn in Scorpio, you travel long and hard through your own personal underworld and bring back gold for the rest of us. What gets in your way is your fear of getting close, but you have to get close and not run when you see someone's dark, ugly, messy, brutal, selfish, ruthless, unpleasant side. You, more than anyone, have the ability to witness someone's shadow and still love them for everything they are.

Your Ambition

You long to not fear death. You long to unite your body and soul with another. You long for commitment and loyalty. You long to face illness and loss with strength. You long to ease the suffering of others.

Do feel your feelings.

Do empathize with others.

Do learn Reiki or other ways to heal.

Don't abandon.

Don't take advantage.

Don't keep score.

If you have a Saturn in Scorpio person in your life, encourage them to investigate their obsessions as well as their repulsions and fears.

Give the Saturn in Scorpio child mysteries and problems to solve. Encourage their intuition. Who took the last cookie? Have them guess! Give them games like Operation and Monopoly. Teach them the value of money and the sacredness of the human body, even at a young age.

Let your child know that the body isn't bad or dirty. Saturn in Scorpio may hate or fear it. At the same time, teach your child that it's okay to feel however and whatever they feel. Sometimes even wallowing is a good thing! The Saturn in Scorpio child has strong emotions about everything. Let them know this is perfectly fine.

Give the Saturn in Scorpio employee projects they can sink their teeth into. You want to get them committed, obsessed. Make sure the projects take time and thought and effort. Scorpio is competitive, but Saturn in Scorpio will avoid entering the race. They will not grow, however, unless they compete and try to win. Dangle a prize you know they desire and possibly even fear—like a promotion!

Give the Saturn in Scorpio friend lots of one-on-one time with you and share your most private thoughts and secrets. Listen to theirs. Study the stock market together. Read each other's tarot cards. Saturn in Scorpio needs to learn to share and to invest in others, whether through friendship or love or money.

Give your Saturn in Scorpio spouse or partner mind-blowing spiritual sex. It is essential that you have a physical bond with your true love that is more than just physical. Study Tantra. Study sex sorcery. Learn what turns your partner on. Explore taboos together. Share your fantasies! Seek not codependence or independence but interdependence with your partner. Give and receive.

When you have a Saturn in Scorpio person in your life, your job is to let them know that you love them just the way they are. Scorpio people are always shedding skin, dying and being reborn due to personal losses, betrayals, crisis. Saturn in Scorpio will try to halt or resist the soul's need to transform and grow wise. Let your Saturn in Scorpio loved one know that you will never leave their side.

Saturn in Sagittarius: The Explorer

Sagittarius reminds us to have perspective, to consider the meaning of life. While everyone else is seeing the trees and not the forest, admiring the short term and not the wider view, Sagittarius shows up to set us straight with their frank philosophical talk and big-picture thinking. Life is like a highway, says Sagittarius! Vroom, let's go!

Sagittarius needs room to roam, travel, explore. They are naturally optimistic and will cheer you on like no other. Sagittarius sees your potential.

When your Saturn is in Sagittarius, however, you do not see the big picture and the road ahead. Instead, you see what's right in front of your face, the details, the short term, life as we know it rather than how it could be.

One is not better than the other, big picture versus small picture. We need both. We need different things at different times in life, but you, Saturn in Sagittarius, have moments of such puny or narrow vision that some might even mistake you for a Virgo! (Just teasing! I love my Virgos.) Your lack of faith or belief in people, and in the world around you, will sadden not only your dearest friends but yourself as well. You must learn to look up!

When Saturn is in Sagittarius, it adds a sand-bag to the usual Sagittarian balloon-like personality. Sagittarius is ruled by lucky abundant Jupiter, and Jupiter is happy and expansive, fun and lively.

When Saturn is in this sign, however, it's not just gloom that occasionally results but downright despair, and it takes that beautiful Sagittarius optimism and stomps on it.

You must learn to temper your pessimism with sweet vision, to soften your realism with belief in magic and that good things happen and good people exist. Even though life is not a dream, it's not always a nightmare either.

Sagittarius is often accused of being excessive or indulgent with food and drink and good times, and Saturn in Sagittarius can go to the opposite extreme: self-denial. Your lust for life is set too low. No adventure, no open road.

Saturn in Sagittarius hides the truth instead of telling it. The truth is that the world is good *and* bad, heavy *and* light, physical and spiritual. But Saturn in Sagittarius will err on the side of somber sobriety until they learn to tell a different story and become that buoyant balloon.

Your Gift

Saturn in Sagittarius, your gift is your reliability, an underestimated trait. We call and you come.

You promise *and* you deliver. Dependable! You pay the bills, remember the appointments, show up for friends and family when we need you. This isn't boring! This is necessary!

You're there for us with your clearheaded, gentle wisdom. You're not a pie-in-the-sky thinker. No wild goose chases or get rich quick schemes here! You don't need to be taught to slow down and listen and take your time. You're patient, thoughtful, and sane. You stay in your lane.

You are detail-oriented, and you catch the little mistakes before they become big ones. I've known more than one Saturn in Sagittarius who knew exactly how much money they had in the bank and budgeted their cash for each week. I know this can frustrate you because you are given the secretarial tasks, but you're good at them and they're easy for you, despite being tedious. You don't quit until the job is done.

Your Challenge

Dear Saturn in Sagittarius, you must learn to broaden your horizons and seek experience. One way to do this is to travel, to explore other countries. You must leave home and get to know other cultures and customs and people around the world, or even in your own community! To leave home is to leave safety. You must wander and roam. You must see your face in the faces of others in strange places.

You are more than just practical and serious and sober. You are glass three-quarters empty, and you often miss the wonder and beauty of animals and nature because you are too busy working, head buried under papers. You work overtime, and for what? It's not about the money.

You must play, not just work. You must pray, not just worry. Many Sagittarius are risk-taking partygoers, thirsty for fun, but this jovial horsey spirit is dormant in you. Learn adventure. Learn the world. Travel for you shouldn't be a hobby but a way of life.

Your Ambition

You long to feel light, to feel the wind in your hair, to travel the seven seas. You long to be free, to wander the world. If only you could feel joy. You long to make your dreams not a reality but into even bigger dreams! Your dreams *are* big, but Saturn talks you out of them. Be the horse. Be the road.

Do move your body.

Do buy a ticket.

Do spin the big wheel.

Don't mope.

Don't rage.

Don't lie down and die.

If you have a Saturn in Sagittarius person in your life, encourage them to look on the bright side of life. Help them see the big picture. Help them to have faith in themselves and others.

Give the Saturn in Sagittarius child a map. Hang it on the wall. Ask them where they'd like to travel and why! Globes are good too. Have them close their eyes, spin the globe, and see where they land. Read to your child adventurous stories of sailors and explorers and pirates. Expose them to different ethnicities and cultures through museum visits and cultural events and festivals. Learn a foreign language together. Model for them a positive, optimistic attitude. Be their cheerleader. Ask them what they're curious about. What do they want to explore?

Give the Saturn in Sagittarius employee less structure, not more. Their best ideas arise when they have freedom and space to create. Your Saturn in Sagittarius employee will insist upon structure and rules anyway, but you don't need to provide it. They do it themselves! Saturn in Sagittarius has vision, but first they need to feel safe.

They are great at dreaming up projects or taking others' ideas and launching the next step. They also analyze where others have gone wrong and then do it better. Reverse engineering! Have them work with the international office and clients from all around the world. Choose them first for travel.

Give your Saturn in Sagittarius friend your open mind. Don't try to convert them. Accept them for who and how they are, whatever they do or don't believe. That said, you can help expand their outlook by sharing with them how you think and what you feel—about everything! Don't be afraid to share your opinions. That's what a true Sagittarius does!

Share with your friend any cultural or religious traditions you have. They will be curious! Go to an international film festival together. Saturn in

Sagittarius likes to stick close to what they know, but their lessons lie in expanding their world.

Give your Saturn in Sagittarius spouse or partner your most encouraging words. Cheer them on. Be their best friend! Tell them that dreams really can come true. Tell them you see their true nature and you love it! Saturn will depress Sagittarius's natural hopefulness, but as their true love, you can break through these blocks and show them the way out of the dark. Travel together. Dream together.

If you have a Saturn in Sagittarius person in your life, tell them you believe in them no matter what! Potential can become reality in the blink of an eye. No dream is too big for Saturn in Sagittarius. Saturn is structure and Sagittarius is the voyager. Get them out in the world. Sail, wander, roam.

Saturn in Capricorn: The Boss

I never knew a Capricorn who didn't work hard. Work themselves to death really. They can make themselves sick with how much they work. They sever their mind-body connection and all sense of balance. Work, work, work. This work, work, work can bring them success and accolades, but at what price? Sanity? Health? Sometimes!

If your Saturn is in Capricorn (and Saturn is the ruler of Capricorn), you have tremendous potential for success, and you're actually very ambitious. The problem is that your brooding and worries get in the way. You torment yourself: Am I on the right path? Am I on the wrong path? Am I too tough? Not tough enough? These sound like "normal" Capricorn Sun worries but believe me, it's magnified when Saturn too is in this sign.

Capricorn has self-doubt, yes, but climbs the mountain of success, mountain after mountain. Goal after goal. Achievement is their middle name. When your Saturn is in Capricorn, you hesitate. That mountain over there? It's *so* big! You worry too much. You have moments when you feel weak and afraid, and this can make you controlling rather than *in control*. Big difference. You may excel in your profession but fear the mountain of relationship, the mountain of love, of family, of self-development. There are all kinds of ways not to climb.

As with Saturn in all the signs, you have a job to do, lessons to learn, and your lessons are Capricorn lessons. Less fret and more stiff upper lip. Less in touch with your every mood and more get the job done. Steady. Capricorn Sun keeps their cool. Saturn in Capricorn needs to learn this.

When your Saturn is in Capricorn, you *must* find your place, home, in the world of work. Even if you are a stay-at-home mom or dad you still must work for money. Capricorn, to fulfill the nature of Capricorn, must make a living, but Saturn will try to scare you away from this task. Persist you must.

You don't want to be the boss but must learn to be the boss, learn to be in charge without worrying what others think. Capricorns can be tough, yes, but they are tough with wisdom and integrity. Being the boss is not the same as being bossy.

Dear Saturn in Capricorn, you will learn to stay strong when things go wrong.

Your Gift

Your gift is your nurturing nature, but you nurture with teeth. You love like a fierce protective mama or papa bear, pushing away any and all who would threaten you or your keep. You defend and protect not only your family but also any vulnerable soul you meet. I have known Saturn in Capricorn soldiers and sailors who excelled at standing watch, guarding people and possessions and plans from day until night and back again.

Your arms—no, your entire body and soul—were made for keeping us safe. Generous and giving, when you love, you love 100 percent and don't hold back. Your supportive and comforting disposition is a blanket of peace for your closest confidants. Your friends become family.

Saturn in Capricorn, we need you on our side. In you, we feel safe and at home.

Your Challenge

How to take charge without being dictatorial? How to be the boss without being bossy? This is your challenge. You're great at feeding us and loving us, but you lose your footing when it's time to put your foot down! You don't trust your own power, so you will push too hard. You don't trust what you believe is true, so you will over-discipline or not discipline enough.

Another challenge for you, Saturn in Capricorn, is that sometimes you simply give too much. Some may even say that you aren't tough enough and that you give until you're empty and sore and have nothing left. You have days, months, years where you spend your energy and your money without thinking. Learn to save. Learn to wait.

Life is not a sprint but a marathon, and often, you expect results too soon. Impatient! Life takes time and your goals and ambitions also do. They need time to simmer. You will value the results far more if they don't arrive immediately. Capricorn knows and respects this, but Saturn in Capricorn will learn it.

Your Ambition

You long to be strong. You *are* strong. You long to be the boss. You *are* the boss! You long to get the job done, but is it the right one? You long for a life of honor. You have one.

Do save for a rainy day.

Do leave home.

Do act your age.

Don't mope.

Don't let your emotions boss you around.

Don't avoid the mountain!

If you have a Saturn in Capricorn person in your life, try to help them find their purpose, help them find their life's work.

Give the Saturn in Capricorn child responsibility at a young age. Age appropriate at first, but then see how they do. They may be ready for more! How can they help you around the house? Let them earn money or treats for their labor. Teach them the value of earning and saving. When I was a child I had a "restaurant," complete with menu, and I would offer to serve my mother breakfast in bed for a few coins! Capricorn is associated with big business, but Saturn in Capricorn will not be ambitious—at first!

Encourage games or make-believe where your child plays teacher or parent or law enforcement, CEO. You want authority and ability to feel familiar to them, not foreign.

Give the Saturn in Capricorn employee a management role. Put them in charge of others right away, but continue to supervise. While they are leading the team, make sure they are leading but not bullying.

Your Saturn in Capricorn employee needs to feel committed not only to the team, but also to the job, the company, and to you. You can create a loyal, conscientious worker out of Saturn in Capricorn once they lose some of their initial fear of messing up. They also likely have had trouble finding the best job position or field for themselves, despite their obvious expertise. You can help them figure it out and then figure out how they can best serve the company.

Give your Saturn in Capricorn friend your ear. Listen to them moan and groan about their worries and problems. That's what friends are for! Your Saturn in Capricorn friend will be there for you too. You can listen to their feelings and offer support while showing them how to be strong. Give them examples from your own life, such as when you conquered a fear. Remind them of their capability, even though they often feel at the mercy of their hurricane-like emotions. Saturn in Capricorn will learn to keep calm and carry on, and as their friend, you can point out that you've seen their fearless core firsthand and that it's fine to sometimes put feelings aside and be tough, be firm.

Give your Saturn in Capricorn spouse or partner a map. Help them discover their life purpose. Since you know your true love the best, you can help them more than anyone.

Without knowing her or his life purpose, Saturn in Capricorn will be miserable. *They must find it.* Capricorn needs their goals and ambitions and mountains to climb, even if it takes years to know which mountains. But you, as their partner, have a sacred role to play. Help them find their mountain! Tell them it won't be easy or quick. Tell them this is the Capricorn way, and Saturn in Capricorn must learn it. Slow, patient, persistent effort!

Saturn in Capricorn may want the easy way out or prefer someone else to do the job, until they begin to integrate Capricorn characteristics. Don't let this happen. Don't do their work for them.

If you have a Saturn in Capricorn person in your life, tell them that Saturn is a promise. Saturn promises that effort is a requirement in this life, and that the payoff, mastery and achievement, is a pleasure unlike any other. It's the payment for a job well done. Emotions don't make them weak but make them wise.

Saturn in Aquarius:
The Unique

Aquarius has charisma. If you are wondering who that glittering magnetic person is with all the people crowding around them, it's likely an Aquarius in your midst, Sun or Rising or even an Aquarius Moon. They are the originals of the zodiac, the unique ones. Innovators. They think for themselves.

Don't you dare tell an Aquarius what to do, unless you want them to do the exact opposite. They do as they please and can be very stubborn, even rigid. They are interesting, social, charming.

If your Saturn is in Aquarius, however, you will be antisocial. You will likely be just as charming and charismatic as the rest of the Aquarians, but you don't want to hold court like they do or sample every party on a given Saturday night. You will be more private and more quiet. In fact, there's a bit of the homebody about you.

You don't want anyone to know how unique you truly are, how independent, how different. And I mean different in a good way.

Truth: You are not like everyone else, and whereas the Aquarius Sun wears this character-istic proudly or without apology, you, Saturn in Aquarius, are uneasy about it. You don't like it. You fear it. It makes you uncomfortable. You'd rather pass for "normal," even if you and your loved ones know otherwise. God forbid anyone call you quirky, eccentric, weird. In your younger years, you were bullied because of your fondness for wearing both stripes and polka dots together or for being oddly good at algebra.

Remember that Saturn creates doubt and hesi-tation in the sign it's in. Your job, Saturn in Aquar-ius, is to embrace your inner freak and through embracing your inner freak, help others embrace theirs. And I mean freak in a good way!

Once you stop being so afraid of your own uniqueness and embrace your authentic self in all its glory, your entire world opens up. Until you do this deeply, until you enroll in Saturn school, you remain in the wrong job, wrong profession, wrong relationship. You may even have the wrong friends, wrong house, wrong country.

Aquarius is a genius and you are too, but you know it makes you stand out, so you hide it, play dumb, pretend you don't think about what you really think about, pretend you don't know what you really know. It will get better as you get older and you find your tribe, your true friends, and your direction in life.

Try not to fight who you are, Saturn in Aquarius. You have so much to teach us, so much knowledge and understanding. Although you risk being ostracized for being yourself, what's just as likely to happen is that you will acquire not only fans and followers but also friends galore.

Your Gift

Saturn in Aquarius, you are loyal. You are steadfast. You have an old-fashioned sense of honor, like the cowboys in black-and-white movies. These qualities make you a dependable friend and faithful partner. You're not interested in what everyone else is doing or wearing or saying. You're not a gossip. You refuse to scatter your energy. You know how to be here now.

You are also, potentially, the best teacher of the zodiac. You have an innate ability to explain the most esoteric or abstract concepts, from physics to reincarnation. You break these topics down into simple language that anyone can understand. You explain things, and the light bulb goes off in our heads: *Aha,* we cry! *I get it now!* The thing is this, though: you feel the most comfortable when you are explaining others' ideas, rather than your own.

You have another incredible gift that I almost don't want to mention, but I will. You would make a great spy. You hide in plain sight. If the FBI or CIA are hiring, you should send in your résumé. No matter what's going on inside of you, in your head or your heart, you have an uncanny ability to blend in and fit in. You own and cultivate a mask of normalcy, and it can take years for others to see the real you, if they ever do. Will you let them?

Your Challenge

Saturn in Aquarius, you are afraid to be Aquarius. Saturn fears. Saturn doubts!

What is Aquarius? Friendly! Social! Intellectual! Stubborn! Brilliant! So you, Saturn in Aquarius, must hone these qualities. You must not stay at home all the time. You must not stick to one or two friends but branch out.

You must not read the same book over and over but constantly expand your knowledge. You must not always go with the flow but instead hold fast to your beliefs and habits. Do not always be like the branch, but instead be the trunk of the tree, harder to cut down or fall. You must do all these things because Saturn is your teacher (this is true for us all!) and has lessons for you, Aquarius lessons. Aquarius is the genius of the zodiac. Do not be afraid of your wild mind!

It's okay to think for yourself. It's okay to have your own ideas. It's okay to not be like everyone else. It's okay to *not* hide your uniqueness and unicorn horn and who you truly are. It's okay to follow your own rules rather than the rules others have set. It's okay to be an *individual* and to encourage others to do the same.

Your Ambition

You long to be like everyone else. You are not like everyone else. You long for the status quo. You should reject the status quo. You long to follow the rules but also to create the rules. Do both!

Do set the trends.

Do be you.

Do think outside the box.

Don't follow fashion.

Don't stay at home.

Don't fear your wild mind.

If you have a Saturn in Aquarius person in your life, your job is to champion their individuality.

Give your Saturn in Aquarius child unusual games and toys. The weirder, the better! They may be ready for older kids' toys even when they are still young. Buy them books. They will read early.

Definitely set up play dates to encourage early socialization. Aquarius is extroverted, but Saturn in Aquarius will have a shy streak.

You want your Saturn in Aquarius child to make friends with their own mind. They will show proof of genius at a young age. Help them be comfortable with this. Tell them their uniqueness is a gift and some-day they can share it with the world if they choose. They may invent a machine that makes all of our lives easier or discover a cure for the common cold.

Give the Saturn in Aquarius employee the opportunity to invent something new, a new product, a new way of implementing or managing. Original projects only. Don't just let them edit what others have already done. They have to create!

Your Saturn in Aquarius employee may try to hide in his or her office, but you have to put them with the group. Put him or her on a team. They will bring out the best in others while standing out themselves as someone special.

And give them the freedom to create their own schedule. The more they can set their own rules, the happier and more productive they will be. Saturn in Aquarius can predict trends so don't forget to ask their opinion about your latest launch!

Give your Saturn in Aquarius friend an astrology reading as a gift. They likely are fascinated by astrology and have other New Age or occult interests. Share your social life with them. Introduce them to your friends. Although Aquarius loves to connect with others and is good at it, Saturn in this sign can make them overly reclusive, and they could become lonely.

Above all, let your Saturn in Aquarius friend know that their "crazy" ideas are fine with you, and you want to hear more. One of those ideas may be a winner, a moneymaker, the solution to the world's troubles.

Give your Saturn in Aquarius spouse or partner the freedom and space to be themselves. Never judge. They may not take this freedom and space on their own, although they need it. You can gently back away when you feel them going within. The wall will go up. It's not hard to detect. But then it will come down. They need you whether they tell you or not.

Saturn in Aquarius is a secret eccentric, a secret mad scientist, and Saturn will create a feeling of shame or guilt about this. Never call them strange or weird. What they are is who they are, your loving partner whose destiny it is, not to think outside the box, but to dismantle the box totally. Saturn in Aquarius needs to know that you love them no matter what, especially as they take steps to show the world who they truly are.

If you have a Saturn in Aquarius person in your life, you have met brilliance, but with a catch. They are going to want to hide it. They are going to pretend to be like everyone else until they learn the lessons Saturn has for them. Your job is to let them know that who they are is *perfect* and that their glittering genius is their gift to the world.

Saturn in Pisces:
The Dreamer

Saturn in Pisces can't be Pisces. Saturn in Pisces refuses to be Pisces. Saturn throws up a block, a lock, a restriction, and bam! No Pisces to be found. Or very little. Bits and pieces.

What is Pisces? Pisces goes with the flow. Pisces is a water sign. Pisces is compassionate. Pisces heals others with their loving mermaid touch. Empathy! Pisces may be flighty or flakey, but it's okay because Pisces can zone out and relax and float and dream and stare out the window and teach us all how to let go. She doesn't judge others. He has a heart of gold.

But when your Saturn is in Pisces you want everything so damn defined and clear and clarified and *perfect* that you stop the flow. Perfect doesn't flow.

When your Saturn is in Pisces, you can become obsessed with facts and figures, with editing your thoughts, with naming and classifying, with correcting others. The truth is, you need to learn to resist this compulsion to fix and solve every person and problem you encounter.

There is a kind of falling apart that the true Pisces has mastered. Call it *surrender*. Surrender to what is. The ideal Pisces Sun or Moon or Rising can radically accept things as they are, which is different than escapism. They surrender while remaining present.

When your Saturn is in Pisces, you don't trust your intuition. Instead, it makes you nervous. For decades you may avoid your own obvious psychic gifts. You may avoid the metaphysical or spiritual despite being drawn to such matters. You will rely on facts but hardly on faith. Remember that Pisces goes with the flow. Pisces loves all. You can't love all and have compassion for all with your logic and mind and intellect. It's impossible. True Piscean love comes only from the heart, from the soul flow.

Saturn in Pisces doesn't want to give, but give they must. Saturn in Pisces is tight, but loosen up they must! Saturn in Pisces is a secret (or not-so-secret) fault-finder and tattletale. This is the opposite of Piscean soul flow love. They become escapist because the pain is too much—their own pain and the pain of the world. It's unbearable. They feel *everything*. Many Saturn in Pisces thus have addiction issues to deal with what they cannot bear to feel.

So how can Saturn in Pisces handle life better? There is only one solution: to let the feelings wash over them, cleanse them, drench them, instead of letting Saturn stop the flow. Only the healing waters can heal Saturn in Pisces.

Saturn is a locked door, a dam, and Pisces is the water. Once Saturn unlocks the door, once the levee breaks, the feelings and the intuition rush in fully and completely.

Your Gift

Saturn in Pisces, you have a fine critical mind. You're an intellectual powerhouse. Smarty-pants! People come to you for advice whether or not you feel qualified to give it. You discern. You judge. In fact, people may be afraid of you because of this sharp mind.

You're a writer and a thinker, and we need your kind of clarity and certainty in the world. You also run to help others. You're quick to give your astute guidance.

And no matter how dreamy you appear to be sometimes, you live firmly in reality, in the here and now. You know the difference between right and wrong, even if you don't always follow the Golden Rule. You're practical. You easily separate the crucial from the irrelevant, and these judgment calls make you a wise and trusted friend. We trust you even when you don't trust yourself.

Your Challenge

Saturn in Pisces, you must learn to trust the chaos inherent in life, learn to trust the bounce of ocean waves. As the years go by, you will discover that the chaos isn't actually chaos at all, but flow. Up and down, in and out, back and forth. And from that flow you will learn faith and to trust in what you cannot see or understand.

Until you learn to flow, however, you will feel crushed by the reality and demands of the physical world. Making money and taking care of your body, your home, your daily life can be overwhelming.

You will rely on science for all the answers, but science will let you down. You will seek to rely on proof, but proof will let you down. Dear Saturn in

Pisces, you *know* the truth—that there is more to life than meets the eye—but you hardly trust it.

Until you let your feeling flow and allow your intuition to have a say, day in and day out, you will feel uneasy and overwhelmed on this earth. The very thing you fear most—the messy, lawless unpredictable, emotional waves that we *all* have—is the very thing you need.

Your Ambition

You long to feel. You long to not feel submerged when you feel. You long to help others without hating them or feeling resentful, to heal others with just a touch. You long to feel relaxed and willowy, to be a mermaid. You are a mermaid! You need not escape who you are to be who you are!

Do play with tarot cards.

Do give money away.

Do feel your feelings.

Don't fault find.

Don't wait for confirmation.

Don't insist on certainty.

If you have a Saturn in Pisces person in your life, your job is to push them into the pool. But seriously, Pisces is a tender, compassionate water sign. Help them not be afraid of their sensitivity.

Give the Saturn in Pisces child games without rules, games without structure, time to dream, lands of make-believe, imaginary friends, sand castles. Give them time to do nothing at all for a Saturn in Pisces child will be worried about time, even from an early age.

Take your Saturn in Pisces child to the ocean, let them watch the waves come and go. This is the rhythm of life that Pisces understands but Saturn in Pisces finds threatening. Tell them that the waters of life will not swallow them up. They can learn to float, to swim, be *one* with the water. The Saturn in Pisces child needs a little wild water time.

Give the Saturn in Pisces employee a puzzle to wrestle with and solve. Maybe it's a project or problem that everyone else in the office has failed to decode and given up on. At first, Saturn in Pisces may try to use their logic and wise mind to retrieve the solution, but under your encouragement, they may discover that intuitive flashes work best!

The Saturn in Pisces employee will prefer to be detached from the work, from you, from the organization, but you'll get better job performance the more emotionally invested they are. Saturn in Pisces will excel, not only in social work and the helping professions, but also in business. The key is to get them to trust their gut reactions, which they usually have in spades, all day long.

Give the Saturn in Pisces friend a deck of tarot cards. You can trade readings. They will be quite good at it without any study or previous knowledge. Encourage them to explore psychic phenomena or the supernatural and to play in the invisible realms. Saturn in Pisces is a natural skeptic or cynic, but becoming more comfortable with the world of dreams and spirits is essential for learning Saturn in Pisces lessons. They must let down the Saturn guard.

Give your Saturn in Pisces spouse or partner an easy out, an escape route. Rely on them, but let them wiggle away like a fish. Let them sleep in. Give them freedom. Don't mother. Don't smother. Don't overbook your life with them or plan activities or housework or obligation round the clock. They are naturally responsible and need to learn flux and tides and deep breathing. Take a meditation class together or yoga. Go watch the whales. Saturn in Pisces literally can learn from the ocean. Have a second honeymoon in Hawaii. Take a pleasure cruise to parts unknown.

Saturn in Pisces fears the unknown. Saturn in Pisces fears letting go. Your job is to enter the abyss with them. Show them there's nothing to fear.

Chapter 5

Saturn in the Houses

Saturn in the First House

*The First House is associated
with fire sign Aries and the planet Mars.*

Saturn in the First House natives are mature, fiery,
self-starters. They are trustworthy and dependable
and hate to let people down. They will have a take-
charge, dominant flavor to their personality. They
may be bold about it or the strong, silent type. No

matter how it expresses itself, they were born to be the boss.

They are enterprising, but they also respect tradition. They combine creative inspiration with conventional approaches. They may wear a uniform at their nine-to-five job but play the saxophone at an after-hours jazz club on the weekends.

This way, Saturn in the First House has a regular regimented schedule, which makes Saturn happy, but also a fun creative outlet, like music, to satisfy that First House urge for self-expression.

The First House truly is a great place for Saturn for a musician because musicians must practice. Saturn knows that practice is required for success, and Saturn wants success! Also, the First House wants to make a splash in this life. They are not satisfied to play it safe or live life on the sidelines. Saturn will thus be helpful here, slowing down any First House impetuosity and adding in more than a dose of thoughtful planning.

················ *ADVICE* ·················

Don't tell them what to do.

They want to figure it out on their own by trial and error. They are okay with going through this process as Saturn in the First House doesn't need to get it right the first time. They know anything worth having takes patience, and they are willing to learn from their mistakes.

Saturn in the First House natives are old before their time. You may even hear some of them say that they were born old. You can see it in their faces. They have wise eyes, no matter their sparkle or sorrow.

As children, they were likely given responsibilities that far exceeded what was appropriate. They may have had to parent their parent or siblings. This is the typical latch-key child, not necessarily neglected or abused but treated like an adult, and Saturn in the First House kids rise to the occasion as best they can. It's natural for them to assume responsibility for themselves and others, whether or not it is in their best interest. You seldom hear them complain.

The ideal job for the Saturn in the First House person is one where they can work hard, tirelessly even, and exert control or authority over others, and I mean this in a good way. Jobs where Saturn in the First House can protect others is also recommended.

Think police officers, security guards, military jobs, a UN peacekeeper, firemen, inspectors of all kinds. And think of any job where you are paid to be serious! For example, an investigative photo journalist in a warzone delivering hard news and images would be a great career for Saturn in the First House. People with First House planets want an exciting life.

Saturn in the First House has such a serious side to the personality and outlook on life that no matter what else the chart is up to, that serious side will manifest. Remember also that these natives are passionate, so the career, the life, must include these passions. They can't just go to work and go home day after day. All work and no play is a risk for Saturn in the First House.

Saturn in the First House is a grown-up. They can handle grown-up obligations, but they also may have a temper. There's a tendency to be controlling, domineering, even cruel at times. They can be depressive. They can be "too serious" for many people and have trouble relaxing and letting their guard down. They get isolated and feel they have no true friends in the world.

Above all, Saturn in the First House people are always working. They never get a day off, and these natives will benefit from friends and loved ones who can help them see the lighter side of life and get them away from work for a day (or more! Go ahead, try it!). They will be work obsessed, authority obsessed, may be an authority figure themselves, and not take it well when you challenge their tried-and-true approaches to life. Respect them, and you'll have a friend for life.

Dear Saturn in the First House, we know you work hard no matter what. Don't forget to play hard too.

Saturn in the Second House

The Second House is associated with earth sign Taurus and the planet Venus.

Saturn in the Second House works hard for their money. They work hard for every penny. There's no way to make this truth pretty. They may be excellent at their job and at the actual earning, but money doesn't come easy for Saturn in the Second House. Long hours, long days, that phrase "no free lunch" could apply to this Saturn placement. Thus, the Saturn in the Second House person must roll up their sleeves, get to work, and realize this is a life-long condition. It's not a punishment, although it may feel that way sometimes.

That said, it's even more important that Saturn in the Second House find the job and the way to earn money that feels perfect for them because they will have to work themselves to the bone anyway. May as well take the time and apply the effort toward finding exactly what they need, work-wise, and money-wise, to be happy.

· · · · · · · · · · · · · · · · · · · **ADVICE** · · · · · · · · · · · · · · · · · ·

***Don't tell them how to earn their money.
They have to decide for themselves.***

· ·

Remember that Saturn moves slowly. Saturn in the Second House moves slowly multiplied by a hundred. By the time they are in high school or, ideally, earlier, Saturn in the Second House should be on their way to figuring out their ideal career.

Remember too that Saturn is related to our life path as well as to our fate. Saturn in the Second House has a "daily grind" type of fate and won't ever be happy unless this fate is addressed and accepted and the best career for the native is chosen!

There's another example of how Saturn in the Second House can play out. There are people who do not have to work or earn a daily wage to pay their rent or mortgage and bills. They either inherited money or married it, or made it all on their own and retired. They don't have to worry about the money coming in or the money going out. It may not be unlimited, but it can feel that way at times. Well, the Second House doesn't just rule earned income; it also rules our self-worth. You will find Saturn in the Second House people then for whom this issue plays out, not in terms of money in the bank, but esteem, and they will have to work tirelessly hard to grow theirs, to invest in theirs, to have some on hand, plenty to spare, and enough left over, and it will feel like work to them. This process becomes their job. It may take therapy, it may take all manner of callisthenic self-development programs. Just as the worker must roll up their sleeves and get to work, the one who doesn't have to worry about earning money must get to work too.

The ideal job for Saturn in the Second House, then, is one you are madly in love with, a career you stubbornly pursue and never give up. Do not waste your time with lukewarm positions or fake passions or doing what other people think you should do. It will never work except in the short term.

The Second House is associated with the planet Venus, who rules art and beauty and style, so Venus jobs will serve you well and you, them. Finance would also be appropriate as the Second House is one of the money houses.

Some possible job options for Saturn in the Second House include: accountant, financial consultant, stockbroker, set designer, architect, makeup artist, aesthetician, hairdresser, fashion designer, model. You could be a painter, a filmmaker, a sculptor, an arts administrator, the head of a museum. If you are an artist, then you won't just scribble away as a hobbyist; you will have a plan for your art and can make it a *real* career. You may also be a singer as the Second House is associated with the throat.

At its best, Saturn in the Second House will bring discipline to your financial life. You will learn to budget and live within your means. You will save for a rainy day and have plenty left over.

With this placement, you actually can make money. You won't go hungry unless you let the lean months or years (and we all have them) get you down. Saturn will often make us feel like we can't rise to the challenge, but Saturn also bestows power and authority in the house where it is placed, so the truth of the matter is you *can* be the boss of money rather than money or money fear be the boss of you.

At their worst, Saturn in the Second House people don't believe they deserve nice things. Yes, you have to work to earn your daily bread (be it money or esteem), but this doesn't mean you can't enjoy and revel in luxury and pleasure. After all, you earned it!

Saturn in the Second House can take the spartan style to an extreme and never indulge in a silly purchase. They may become obsessed with coupon clipping and sales. And also at its worst, Saturn in the Second House can be stingy with themselves and with others. They can be so afraid of going without, of not having enough, of having to work so hard for everything that they will save it all but never enjoy any of it.

Dear Saturn in the Second House, please don't make your daily grind fate keep you from enjoying the fruits of your labor. Finding work you love will liberate you!

Saturn in the Third House

The Third House is associated with
air sign Gemini and the planet Mercury.

Saturn is serious, and Saturn will display its seriousness wherever it shows up in the birth chart. Saturn
in the Third House, then, is a seemingly contradictory match.

The Third House unadulterated, without the
presence of Saturn, can be fast thinking and fast
talking, the house of writing and communications,
the house of business too. It's a busy house. It talks
with its hands, sometimes nonstop! It can be a little
wild in there.

But Saturn in this house is going to make
communication very serious and possibly molasses
slow. This placement can make a person quiet or
silent, insecure about what they have to say.

On the positive side, since the Third House is
the house of writing, Saturn in the Third House will
be good discipline for writers or those who dream
of writing. It will be easy for them to plan out and
structure their novels, poems, essays. They make
outlines. They love outlines.

On the other hand, their writing won't flow easily or randomly like someone with dreamy Neptune in the Third House, and they probably won't embellish the facts like someone with Jupiter there. Saturn in the Third House is a storyteller, but the stories are most likely the truth, the hard truth, and nothing but.

·················· *ADVICE* ··················

Don't put words in their mouth.
Let them take their time.

··

A Saturn in the Third House writer or thinker will have trouble being spontaneous. Their writings may be too bare bones because Saturn will remove any flourishes that can make writing fun to read. Saturn is not Venus!

The ideal job for a Saturn in the Third House person is a job where they have to focus, where they can put that intense Saturnian concentration to work. Think scientist. Think researcher, writer, or editor, organizing thoughts and words. Saturn in the Third requires jobs for the mind. Any kind of analyst.

Saturn in the Third House people also excel at jobs that require manual dexterity or hand-eye coordination. Saturn in the Third House will stay on task, stay focused, has good hands and a great brain. Think surgeon, artist, welder, administrative assistant—a fast typist, the word processor who never makes a mistake, the painter who can create the most lifelike portraits, mental focus and patience for hours.

At its best, Saturn in the Third House is stable. Saturn takes the busy mind of the scattered Third House and harnesses it. It puts it on a leash. It makes it behave! It gives it something to do! And when Saturn is in charge of the mind itself, the entire life outlook is affected. The result then is someone who takes life seriously, and we in turn take them seriously. As long as they can keep their moods balanced and their spirits uplifted, you will find some of the most reasonable and emotionally healthy people of the whole zodiac.

At its worst, however, Saturn in the Third House can express itself as dark moods and thoughts. The Third House is associated with the mind, so Saturn in the Third House is where we will find not just seriousness but depression. Forget glass half-empty. These natives don't have a glass at all. This isn't true for every Saturn in the Third House, but the tendency is there for the mood to go dark and low and slow. Every natal Saturn in the Third House should watch out for these times of dark clouds.

Another difficult manifestation of Saturn in the Third House is meanness, cruelty. Remember that Saturn is authority, Saturn is in charge, and if you mix it up with the ace communication skills of the Third House, the worst-case scenario is verbal abuse. These are really two sides of the same coin, depression or negative self-talk versus lashing out. Many Saturn in the Third House people need to learn to speak gently—to themselves and to others.

Dear Saturn in the Third House, we know you have trouble looking on the bright side. Let us help you see the sun.

Saturn in the Fourth House

*The Fourth House is associated
with water sign Cancer and the Moon.*

It's impossible to talk about Saturn in the Fourth House without talking about home, family, and the parents or primary caretakers. We also talk about Saturn in this house in more personal ways than Saturn in some of the other houses. It's more psychological, more close to the bone.

The Tenth House/Fourth House axis of the zodiac wheel is often referred to as the parental axis. The Fourth House often represents the mother but sometimes represents the father. It really depends on the particular chart, the person's life experience, and the astrologer who's looking. I don't even decide which house is mother and which house is father until I talk to the person.

And because we are talking about home and family, Saturn in the Fourth House discussions will often revolve around the earlier years, childhood, what life was like at home. Was it happy? Sad? Traumatic? Wonderful? Was there a divorce? Foster care? With Saturn there, we know there was an extra hurdle of some kind, that the early years weren't all roses and butterflies. Similar to Saturn in the First House, this native may have been given responsibilities that they were not ready for or that were not age appropriate, such as caretaking of elders in the household or other jobs that were far more advanced than their tender years. When you hear about a young child who is taking care of their even younger siblings, dressing them for school, cooking all the meals, this may be a Saturn in the Fourth House situation.

•••••••••••••••••• *ADVICE* ••••••••••••••••••

Don't overwhelm them with household duties!

•••

Saturn in the Fourth House can also denote the early death of a parent or caretaker or even neglect of a child. It will sometimes manifest like this because Saturn can be harsh and Saturn can be cruel and the Fourth House is our start in life. On a good day, Saturn is the kind and gentle father or mother who teaches you necessary life skills with patience, but on a bad day, this same Saturn figure metes out unfair punishment.

Saturn in the Fourth House can create an unusually stable household, stable parents, but one where life is very regimented and there are more rules than playdates. The child may have been alone too often for too long.

One thing is for sure, though: With Saturn in the Fourth House, the parents were likely harsher and harder than they needed to be and/or the child experienced them that way. One or both parents expressed Saturn, and the child absorbed it. This Saturn energy then becomes imprinted on the child and they become Saturn, just like the parents. How it ultimately manifests for the child later in life will be different for each person. Will they try to soften some of Saturn's harder edges? Will they become even more harsh? Maybe they will strike a balance.

The ideal job for a Saturn in the Fourth House person is centered around the home, family, kitchen, children. This is where they are comfortably in charge and can excel. Saturn in the Fourth House is no less of a boss than any other Saturn, but here the domain is home related. Think daycare worker, teacher, coach. Think interior design. Gardening or lawn care. Real estate. Anything related to houses. Working from home at any job! Home furnishings. Nanny, parent, housekeeper, house painter. Hotels, motels, and cruise ships (these are temporary homes!).

Saturn is not an emotional planet, not a touchy-feely planet, but the Moon is, and the Moon rules the Fourth House. You see the contradiction. How can Saturn in the Fourth House ever be good?

At its best, the Saturn in the Fourth House person will make an excellent parent or caretaker of family and home. They are an able and confident disciplinarian without sliding into the savage side of Saturn. Saturn in the Fourth House people have boundaries, and they will nurture from a place of strength rather than insecurity. This is the parent who doesn't let the child walk all over them. The roles are clear.

At its worst, Saturn in the Fourth House is the domineering, punishing parent, even abusive, sadistic. It's not that the Fourth House brings out the worst in Saturn. It's that the Fourth House is the setting where Saturn happens. Saturn wants to be at work. Saturn wants to be in the world. Saturn wants recognition for a job well done. Saturn stuck at home, in the private world of the Fourth House, is going to feel frustrated and will take it out on those closest to it.

I want to emphasize that this worst-case scenario isn't a given. You may have Saturn in the Fourth House yourself and be a perfectly loving person who wouldn't hurt a fly if you could help it. What I am describing here is a risk factor.

Dear Saturn in the Fourth House, although your early years were challenging, you have the rest of your life ahead of you. You can heal any old pain and create your dream home.

Saturn in the Fifth House

*The Fifth House is associated
with fire sign Leo and the Sun.*

Saturn in the Fifth House is the artist—the serious artist, not the dilettante. Saturn in the Fifth House is never content to just play or have fun or even enjoy life—which is what the Fifth House is about. The Fifth House is the party, but Saturn adjusts the rules of wherever it is placed. It puts a Saturn stamp on things, the serious stamp!

Remember that Saturn over our lifetime makes an expert of us, so there are Fifth House matters that this native will at first fear and then try to control and then eventually master. Saturn always has a job to do and will make us miserable if Saturn can't do that job.

With this placement, you will likely see an aptitude for art and an imaginative child, despite the pursed lips and serious face and eyes of concentrated effort. Those are artistic visions being dreamed up but not with fuzzy Neptune wings. Instead, we find a planner, a budding architect.

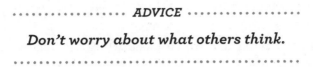

Don't worry about what others think.

Early on, you may have felt self-conscious because you were more serious than the other kids at school or in the neighborhood. You didn't fit it and you probably still don't! But if you have Saturn in the Fifth House or know someone who does, please know that this placement doesn't actually dull your shine. What it does is make you determined to shine even brighter. Saturn in the Fifth House equals determination *plus* natural talent, and this combination is the one that will rise to the top!

The ideal job for the Saturn in the Fifth House person can show up in a few different ways. On the one hand, there's the creative artist track. The Fifth House rules self-expression, and you are thus tasked to be yourself in your work, express yourself, whatever you choose.

Saturn in the Fifth House, remember this: You have to take yourself seriously (don't fight against it!). You eventually *will* take yourself seriously. For years or decades, you could talk yourself out of the work you need to do most of all. Saturn loves to put delays or obstacles in front of us.

Saturn in the Fifth House as the artist is any kind of artist: visual art, conceptual art, theater, writing, photography, graphic design. It's all covered here. The more structure, the better.

Saturn in the Fifth House, like Saturn in the Fourth House, may also choose and excel at a kid-centered profession: teaching, tutoring, daycare, nanny, professor of education, CEO of a toy company.

Then there's the gambler. The Fifth House rules speculation and games and the Fifth House Saturn person could make this a career. Poker champion. Any kind of fun or recreational activity is covered by the Fifth House. Cruise director is another option. Saturn in the Fifth House leads people in fun!

At its best, Saturn in the Fifth House is a lion tamer. What I mean by this is that Saturn is the boss, the CEO, and she can take the unruly creative energy of the Fifth House and shape it, mold it, give it a structure. She takes the wild thing and teaches it, organizes it, whether it's children who need entertaining or grown-ups doing the cha-cha on a cruise to Alaska.

At its worst, Saturn in the Fifth House people have a hard time letting go and enjoying themselves. This house is the house of fun, playful like children are playful. It rules games and parades! Saturn, usually tentative, will make the native here rarely, if ever, in the mood for fun, the proverbial wet blanket, too reserved to smile. While everyone else is at the party or the pool living it up and having a good time, they know there's work that needs doing. Everyone's having fun, but not me, says Saturn, and yet Saturn in the Fifth House doesn't really mind.

If you have Saturn in the Fifth House, it's up to you to figure out what is fun for you, no matter if it's fun for anyone else. Accept your serious nature and then apply your serious nature so that you reach your dreams.

Don't let others get you down. You're not really a wet blanket—you just have an important job to do! Take that discipline and creativity all the way to the bank and up the ladder of success.

Dear Saturn in the Fifth House, you may not have fun like the other kids, but you'll be creating worlds while they're still in diapers.

Saturn in the Sixth House

The Sixth House is associated
with earth sign Virgo and the planet Mercury.

The Sixth House is associated with health and work and routine, and when under the influence of Saturn, these areas of life can become smoothly running machines or chronically sick. "Smoothly running machine" because Saturn at its best creates order and organization and patterns that stick. "Sick" because Saturn at its worst is a merciless, ruthless tyrant who will drive the body and spirit too hard and into exhaustion.

If you have your Saturn in the Sixth House, you may have been a sickly child with many sensitivities or food allergies. Your parents sought out doctors and specialists, even off-the-beaten-path healers to try to help you. You may have had surgeries or even a disease, even cancer. This is Saturn in the Sixth House at its most brutal.

Saturn in this House will make you an expert on the body. You will know yours inside and out because of your struggles with your health and countless doctors' visits. You probably learned how to heal yourself.

People with Saturn in their Sixth House are some of the hardest workers. They simply don't stop working. They feel responsible for their own work at work and for the success of the whole business. This is one way that Saturn in the Sixth House can go wrong, by taking on too much responsibility. When you have Saturn in your Sixth House, you will notice that the boss keeps piling on the work. They know you're good at it and know you will do it, with or without any help.

One ideal career for Saturn in the Sixth House is the medical field. You are an expert diagnostician and confident in your analysis. You would make a great nurse, doctor, chiropractor, paramedic (although paramedic or trauma-related healer might make some Saturn in the Sixth House people too nervous). You would make a great energy healer, like a Reiki master or other modality.

Your body has been acutely sensitive for as long as you can remember, but you can use it like a tuning fork to tune in to others and gain insight into their health issues. Anything you drink or eat, any environment you put yourself in will affect you. You are one of the zodiac's most highly sensitive people. You can be anxious, paranoid, even a hypochondriac at times. As you get older, though, you will learn to tell the difference between anxiety and intuition and to trust your body's impulses and messages. The ideal job for you is one that will help you do this. The more you help others, the more you help yourself.

Another ideal path or job for you is anything related to cleaning or cleansing energy or space, like a witch or shamanic practitioner. In fact, you may already be a witch. You may also be a literal cleaner of houses who loves doing windows, has their own housekeeping business, and can find every single little thing that is wrong with a place. Your eyesight, be it your actual eyes or your third eye, is that good. You may be a master of the smudge stick or master of cleaning cobwebs off ceiling fans. Maybe both! Anything detail oriented is for you. You catch everyone's mistakes.

The Sixth House is also the house of the servant or subordinate, so with Saturn here, you may be the one in charge of all the workers because that is Saturn's way, of course. Saturn takes charge!

At its best, Saturn in the Sixth House brings discipline and structure to one's daily habits, which includes everything from diet to work to workouts, any personal routine. Creating order is easy when Saturn lives in the Sixth but it can be challenging then to try new things.

If you start a diet, you will stick with it. If you decide to clean the house every Tuesday, you will stick with that too. You are the master of routine and rarely skip an obligation. Saturn brings reliability wherever it is, but this quality is extra pronounced in the Sixth House, which is a reliable house even without Saturn there. The Sixth is the datebook, the calendar of the zodiac.

Creating order is easy when Saturn lives in the Sixth House, but it can be challenging to try new things. Problems result when rigidity sets in. The Sixth House should be flexible, able to change its mind despite the schedule and not have everything set in stone. You may need to adjust the way you eat. You may need to clean the house on Wednesday instead of Tuesday. What good is Saturn if we can't ever change our minds or make adjustments? Well, that's not my job, says Saturn.

At its worst, Saturn's influence here can make daily life too inflexible and create fear of changing anything at all, even if it makes you unhappy. We see too many intractable rules, too many structures that have outgrown their use, and definitely too much work. With Saturn in the Sixth House, we find the workaholic who has every stress-related symptom under the sun. We also find autoimmune diseases with this placement and natives who are unable to process their emotions and experiences because the mind is so busy and so is the body. They never truly rest.

Saturn in the Sixth House can create health problems, but you can use your Saturn skill set to create healthy structures for yourself, the diet and sleep and exercise and work that is best for you. Preventive medicine.

Dear Saturn in the Sixth House: you must learn to rest.

Saturn in the Seventh House

*The Seventh House is associated
with air sign Libra and the planet Venus.*

One of the main themes of the Seventh House is the
committed love relationship, and with Saturn in this
house, that special love relationship of your dreams
will be hard to find. For sure, you will get frustrated.
Many of you put in your fair share, *more* than your
fair share of effort, seeking high and low throughout
your life for this elusive love, and the lack of it causes
you pain. *I'm an expert on love,* you think to yourself. *I help my friends with all their love problems.
Why can't I find mine?* But for Saturn in the Seventh
House, this search can take years, even decades.
Saturn delays.

Your standards are high—not too high, but high.
Also, it may not just be a life partner that is delayed.
Close friends can be hard to find, people who can
understand you and see the real you. Why? There
is a reserve (Saturn!) about you. There is a wall. You
have trouble letting people in. It feels so much safer
to keep them at a distance.

Some would even say you have a fear of getting close, that it's more than mere high standards. Fear of commitment. Fear of marriage. Fear of other people. This fear inadvertently makes you push people away because of that overly domineering or authoritative manner. Who wants to get close to that? It's off-putting. You are like a general in the army sometimes. I don't mean to make you feel bad, Saturn in the Seventh House, but I do want to point out to you that some of your own behaviors can get in your way. You're tough.

And although Saturn will try to convince you otherwise, you aren't supposed to avoid relationships. You have your set of lessons just like all the other Saturns. In your case, though, your lessons are intimately involved with other people. You can't live life on your own all alone, even though this may be your instinct or desire, especially when you realize how complicated people are!

Alternatively, another way this can show up is the Saturn in the Seventh House person who has no trouble finding love or close friendship but takes their love or friendship *very* seriously. When they commit they commit for life and they never ever stray. True blue! Saturn in the Seventh House can also be an older partner, or you may be the older partner. Or it may not be an age difference but a difference in maturity. With Saturn in the Seventh House, one of you is the Saturn, older, wiser, and in charge.

On the even gloomier side, a natal Saturn in the Seventh House can represent the death of the partner or a difficult marriage, difficult partner, illness. There will be some kind of hardship or harshness to the relationship, including choosing someone who will be abusive. Although these are worst-case scenarios, it sometimes does happen.

·················· **ADVICE** ··················

Don't give up on love.

Don't give up on finding the partner of your dreams, no matter how long it takes. It's your destiny to search and find and become an authority, not only on the search for love, but also on the manifestation for yourself! Saturn rules time. We are always forced to take our time when Saturn is involved. Saturn won't refuse you forever.

An ideal job for Saturn in the Seventh House is one where you can help couples or coworkers make peace: smoothing over troubled relationships, helping with negotiations between disagreeing people. Think marriage counselor. Think advice columnist. Think diplomat! Yes, Saturn in the Seventh House can even make peace between warring nations! Your rational, objective nature brings calm solutions to even the most tense deliberations.

At its best, Saturn in the Seventh House is the loyal partner and worker, mature and reliable. You look before you leap, never rushing, and wait for the right time to commit, be it personal or professional.

Problems come when you wait too long and miss opportunities. Saturn in the Seventh House at its worst will drag its heels and slow down process to a snail's pace. And while you are busy filibustering and slowing things down, you may blame the other person for being difficult! Too bossy or too domineering are some of the criticisms hurled at you, but you can soften these hard edges. You just have to stay aware of the tendency. Easier said than done? Of course! But it wouldn't be Saturn if it weren't!

The more you temper Saturn's coldness and the more you emphasize Saturn's calm, plus add in a little sugar, the better you will feel and the better your results will be.

Dear Saturn in the Seventh House, you are the relationship expert, but your job is to take your own advice.

Saturn in the Eighth House

> *The Eighth House is associated with water sign Scorpio and the planet Pluto.*

One prominent theme of the Eighth House is the occult and paranormal.

People with planets in this house will have an interest in these topics and may very well have abilities as well. Saturn's presence here definitely signifies both of these—interest and ability—but also that typical Saturn fear or hesitation, that you wouldn't be good at them or that you should stay away.

You may feel like there's a wall or barrier between you and the Eighth House or that you can never quite find the time to pursue these studies. And of course, since we are talking Saturn, one of your jobs in this life is to become an expert authority on these deep, spooky realms. You may become a talented psychic or medium or ghost hunter. You may become a researcher or detective or teacher of these mysteries. One thing is for certain: once you overcome your hesitation and make friends with your obsession, you will go far.

The question is: Are you brave enough? The Eighth House is not for the faint of heart, and Saturn's influence will not make it easy on you. Although you have intuitive knowledge and skill, you will train. You will want to train. Saturn always does.

If you have Saturn in the Eighth House and are reading this, you may not even believe me that you can achieve this. That's how strong Saturn is—but the Eighth House pull is also strong! The Eighth House is obsessive and compulsive, and even the presence of stalwart Saturn can't stop what is meant to be.

········· *ADVICE* ·················

You have to put Saturn to work and take responsibility for your own damn head and third eye.

··

I know it can be overwhelming. If you have psychic abilities, you may get dark and creepy visions because the Eighth House can be a dark and creepy place, associated with the taboo and with death. For example, you can walk into a room and pick up on all the bad vibes, even bad things that happened years ago. Centuries! You'll feel it. You'll see things.

But if this area of life interests you and draws you to it, don't be scared off. You can learn to work with the energies. You can learn to master them instead of them mastering you. And honestly, it's not like the vibes or visions will leave you alone, whether or not you pursue the occult or paranormal as a career or even as a hobby.

In your early years, you may have gotten yelled at because you predicted when Aunt Irma would die. Or you knew where someone left their car keys, or you spoke the truth when the adults around you told their white lies. You knew too much, you spoke your truth, but then you learned to be quiet and hide your gifts so that you would stop getting punished for talking too much. You brought the shadow, the secret, out of hiding.

The ideal job for Saturn in the Eighth House is the detector of secrets and discoverer of the hidden. Think psychologist. Think psychic, medium, talking to the dead. Think any kind of investigator. Think geologist who studies what lies beneath the earth's surface. You may not be able to see it, but the Eighth House Saturn can, and likely wants to.

The Eighth House has other meanings as well. It's one of the money houses, so Saturn in the Eighth House is a natural accountant or prudent financial advisor. The Eighth House is also associated with sex, so you could combine it with psychoanalysis and be a sex therapist. You could teach people how to be intimate or to have orgasms. It's the house behind closed doors, the stuff we won't talk about in "polite" company. This is your area of expertise when Saturn is in the Eighth House.

At its best, Saturn in the Eighth House gains mastery over these hidden realms and thus is able to help and heal people. Lord knows we all need help with our money and our sex lives and our fear of dying. These are taboo topics, and you are a courageous leader for us through the underworld. You are the tour guide, psychopomp, through what we fear most, reducing our fears as you stand beside us.

At its worst, Saturn in the Eighth House will avoid all those things they must master, like money management, like the meaning of sex, like fear of death, the occult, emotional/spiritual intimacy and bonding. Instead of digging deep, you flee. And flee some more. It is natural and normal for Saturn's presence here to restrict your mastery and restrict your power. You will refuse to die (i.e. refuse to transform) and make the process from novice to adept take much longer than it needs to.

Dear Saturn in the Eighth House, you see and you do what no one else can. Please don't give up.

Saturn in the Ninth House

The Ninth House is associated with fire sign Sagittarius and the planet Jupiter.

One main theme of the Ninth House is the teacher, the educator, schooling, in particular higher education. We already know Saturn is a teacher and an expert, and so is the Ninth House.

When we see any planets in this house at all, we will often find a teacher, be it a teacher of kids or college-age students or continuing education for seniors. Ninth House teachers may not be classroom teachers, though, but teachers of life, the wise friend who gives you advice.

Saturn here, however, creates the teacher who doesn't want to teach, at least not at first. He or she is the reluctant teacher. It can take years for Saturn in the Ninth House people to grow into their fate, which is the rule of Saturn overall. Saturn is the thing we are supposed to become, and likely will become, and yet Saturn always makes us wait. The resistance is built in.

Remember that Saturn is traditional, so once you do become a teacher (I promise that you will, in one form or another), you will likely be interested in teaching in a traditional kind of way or teaching traditional topics, often giving respect to the teachers you yourself learned from. You are part of a lineage and it feels right to you to talk about it. What is a traditional topic? Anything that has stood the test of time. Anything with history—architecture, philosphy, the sciences! Such topics have been studied and taught through the ages.

Also remember that Saturn is the disciplinarian of the zodiac, so you will be a strict teacher, giving rules and grades, no matter how friendly you actually are outside the classroom. Your students may fear you! And no matter how insecure you feel on the inside, please know that Saturn in the Ninth

House was born to teach, and despite the presence of that little, or loud, voice that tries to refuse your fate, you actually are great at it. The fear is as strong as your natural aptitude.

In your early years, people were afraid of you. You have always had a managerial or commanding style to your personality, even if you were a quiet introvert. This probably didn't go over well as a kid when you were supposed to have fun and not be an expert. You may have been a know-it-all or teacher's pet, mature for your age. Too smart! You were the teacher even when there was a teacher, maybe even correcting the teacher! Even if you didn't know much about a particular topic, you sounded confident, maybe bossy, and this could make less secure individuals nervous. They felt, and still feel, threatened by you, that you know more than they do or want to take over.

Not all Saturn in the Ninth House people are reluctant teachers, and not all of them are strict. Some of them embrace their fate early on in life with a smile. All of them, however, have an air of knowledgeable self-confidence whether in their families or at work or in actual classrooms. They just seem to *know,* and others come to them for guidance, even when they were children!

You can't please everyone, so please just be yourself.

Yes, you may alienate others because of your natural self-assurance, but don't let it dissuade you from sharing your expert opinions.

The Ninth House is an expressive house; it's outwardly focused, so an ideal job for Saturn in the Ninth House will be one where you can talk and share, preach and teach, especially if you are sharing not just your own ideas, but the ideas of others. Think teacher of world religions. You would be sharing customs and ritual and history and what people believe.

The Ninth House is an intellectual house but also a passionate house, so as long as you are teaching subjects you feel strongly about, whatever they are, you are on the right track. You want to make people smarter. You want to make people think. You could be an author, a publisher, a travel blogger. Through you, they explore unknown worlds. The Ninth House is associated with international travel and writing and gaining new perspectives.

At its best, Saturn in the Ninth House is tolerant. You have an open mind, are antiracist, and you teach these principles too. Your gift for teaching should not be underestimated by you or anyone else. You may feel like you aren't enough, that you are "just a teacher," but without teachers like you, the world will never get better. On a personal level, you help people more than you ever know. Yes, you may get weary from all the requests for advice, but they wouldn't ask if you weren't the one with the answers.

At its worst, Saturn in the Ninth House thinks they know everything, and they want everyone to know that they know everything! You may feel you have nothing to learn and that no one can school you.

You can be stubborn, dogmatic, even fanatic. You may be too strict, take Saturn past the point of all reason. You may follow the rules just because they are the rules, rather than question them. You may follow tradition or custom even when it's no longer the right approach.

None of us ever stop learning, but Saturn in the Ninth House needs to understand that that eternal student model is actually a good thing so that new ideas and information and attitudes can come in and shake up the old guard. With Saturn in the

Ninth House, you may be that eternal student who goes for degree after degree.

Dear Saturn in the Ninth House, add a little love to your teaching style. You won't lose your students by being nice. In fact, you will win them over. Seduce instead of punish.

Saturn in the Tenth House

The Tenth House is ruled by earth sign Capricorn and the planet Saturn.

Every house on the zodiac wheel has a sign and a planet that is associated with it. Saturn rules the Tenth House. The Tenth House is Saturn's land, his happy place. He's at home here. Saturn is serious. The Tenth House is serious. Saturn is ambitious. The Tenth House is ambitious. The Tenth House itself rules career. Folks with their Saturn in the Tenth may be destined for fame and possibly fortune, and it is a fortunate placement if you are willing to take fate by the horns! Saturn never lets us be lazy, but Saturn in the Tenth House especially will feel burdensome if you don't work it and work for it.

When you see Saturn in someone's Tenth House, what you are seeing is the ultimate career man or woman. Big ambition, big dreams, big job, big mountains to climb, no stopping them. It's a lot to require of one human being, and yet they exist! If you have your Saturn in the Tenth House, you are destined to be a career powerhouse and maybe even to change the world.

Even though Saturn is so at home in this house, we will often still see the usual Saturnian delays. It can take the native a long time to find the perfect career, but they never give up despite all the false starts and obstacles along the road to success.

Similar to Saturn in the First House or Saturn in the Fourth House, as a child you may have felt the weight of the world on your shoulders. One or both of your parents may have been career driven, just like you. One or both of your parents may have been overly strict or overbearing. You may never have felt the love you needed, so career success becomes a substitute.

Saturn's drive and ambition isn't just a substitute for love, although it can show up that way in some lives. Just be aware if you have this placement that love is love and work is work, and work may not fulfill all of your heart's desires.

With natal Saturn in the Tenth House, career confusion blossoms into career certainty over time. They need this blossoming. If they aren't climbing the ladder of success, they feel lost. And once they finish with one ladder, they find another. It hardly matters what else is happening in their lives—be it family or love or children or any interest or hobby or passion—when career is all wrong, when their career is careening out of control, then their life feels out of control. And an out-of-control Saturn is an unhappy Saturn. We all need to find the right work, we all need to find the right way to spend our time and live our lives, but Saturn in the Tenth House has a calling unlike any other. What is this call? To reach the top. They will work for it, yes, but the top is where they are headed.

Will there be fear? Will there be delays? Of course! But they keep going up, up, up, up.

I don't believe there is any one ideal job for Saturn in the Tenth House. The most important thing for Saturn there is to realize its nature. Surrender to it. Accept it. That they won't ever be happy with a "little" job or a "little" place in life. They need to be rock stars in the field of their choice (although perhaps not literal rock stars). Anything less will feel like a loss, and if this is not acknowledged, they will never have the strength to keep climbing. Know thyself, Saturn in the Tenth!

They probably won't be happy as a housewife or househusband. Not that there is anything wrong with either of these roles, but Saturn in the Tenth House wants to express itself in the world. You can't be famous only at home, says Saturn in the Tenth House. The world needs to see you, to know you, to realize your expertise, your prowess. Perhaps even to worship you. Everyone needs to know how hard you've worked and what you've accomplished.

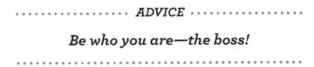

···················· **ADVICE** ····················

Be who you are—the boss!

At their best, Saturn in the Tenth House people change the world and protect the world, no matter the career they choose. They are the holders of power. They set policy and make decisions that affect us all. Yes, they can be conservative. Yes, they may take only calculated risks. Yes, they are ethical, faithful leaders. You will find them in politics but also in the arts and entertainment industry. You will also find them at home, ignoring their calling.

At its worst, Saturn in the Tenth House is so single-minded that they ignore everything and everyone but career, and thus everything and everyone but career will suffer. They will forget to come home for dinner. They will forget to kiss their spouse goodbye. They will miss out on their son or daughter's graduation or ball game because work takes precedence. Neglectful? Sometimes. And when you try to take that career back home? You are in for a fight. The bedroom is not the boardroom, and Saturn in the Tenth House too often tries to solve problems with power and pushiness rather than care and cooperation. You have a one-track mind and a one-track life.

Dear Saturn in the Tenth House, you will go far. Just don't forget the people who love you.

Saturn in the Eleventh House

The Eleventh House is ruled by air
sign Aquarius and the planet Uranus.

One of the main themes of the Eleventh House is friendship, and thus an Eleventh House Saturn may be a lonely Saturn. Saturn makes things hard for us, and in the Eleventh House we can feel disconnected, like a face in the crowd, no matter how many friends and loved ones we have.

The Eleventh House is also the house of hopes and dreams, so you are required to not only explore but also to define and refine what you most want. You can't get it if you don't know what it is, says the Eleventh House. And with Saturn here? You may have one dream in particular that you cling to, even though the door keeps slamming in your face. You don't need to let go of it, though. Keep trying, says Saturn. Don't give up.

What is most deep in your heart? Are you afraid to look? What do you want more than anything? Saturn in the Eleventh House must figure this out, and yes, there will be times when you feel there's no hope for you, but that's just bad Saturn whispering in your ear. A big part of your life path is to figure this out without letting Saturn fear block you. Part the curtains. See what's there. No fear. Yes you may be a loner in the great wide open of the Eleventh House, but remember the Eleventh House is social. It's a people house! You will have to learn to be among them, at least a little, to achieve your dreams.

In your early years, you realized how different you were, different from the other kids. Here in the Eleventh House we find the quintessential outsider who is at home nowhere. If you learned how, you were able to fit in just enough to avoid being bullied, but I think kids always know when there is someone "different" in their midst. They respected you, though. You are a trendsetter. Your mind is fantastic. You think up strange inventions or different ways of doing things. Even as a child, you did this. You probably started a hundred imaginary businesses in a single day. And you knew things before they happened. And you bossed your peers around, which some of them liked and some of them didn't.

· · · · · · · · · · · · · · · · *ADVICE* · · · · · · · · · · · · · · · ·

*Be yourself! You will do it
better than anyone else!*

Ideally, Saturn in the Eleventh House can run a company because the Eleventh House is concerned with networks or associations of people, rather than our more personal interactions. Saturn here sits high on the mountaintop, overseeing the operation as a whole. Think president of a nonprofit or university or large publishing house or bank. Any business will do, but the more humanitarian, the better. A charitable foundation. And the more employees and volunteers, the better. The Eleventh House is a collective, a group, and Saturn in the Eleventh House wants a wide reach. Saturn in the Eleventh House wants to father an organization.

At its best, Saturn in the Eleventh House brings structure and direction to what you most wish for. Saturn will help you break down the plan and think clearly. Can you really have it? Does the plan have holes? What needs to be adjusted? Your dreams and your goals are your friends with Saturn in the Eleventh House. And as long as you don't let your fears stop you, you will absolutely get what you want.

At its worst, Saturn in the Eleventh will let loneliness get in the way of ambition. You believe you can't discuss your true desires with anyone; they wouldn't understand, or maybe they would steal your ideas! Thus, you keep your mouth shut and keep plugging away. You try to believe in yourself even without the support of others. This particular Saturn test can defeat even the most courageous

Saturn in the Eleventh House person because you fear what others think of you.

Saturn in the Eleventh House will also follow too many old rules when what's really needed is a total rewriting and rewiring of the plan. They become too rigid when what they really need is to change course entirely.

Dear Saturn in the Eleventh House: Listen to your life. Is it time for a reinvention?

Saturn in the Twelfth House

The Twelfth House is associated with water sign Pisces and the planet Neptune.

This is a tough one. It just doesn't make sense. And yet there are people who have Saturn in the Twelfth House, of course. What's it all about? Remember that Saturn pulls things together. Saturn makes life concrete. Saturn loves the law!

But in the Twelfth House? No law, no concrete, no pulling things together. Instead, Saturn dissolves. Saturn disperses. Structure goes slack. And yet the Twelfth House is more than an ocean of chaos. The

Twelfth House is the most mystical and spiritual of the houses. There is order there, just a different kind of order than Saturn prefers. So what happens when Saturn lives in the murky Twelfth House?

Although Saturn will definitely lose its footing and some of its major meanings in key ways, when Saturn is in this house, it will gain new substance and new meaning. Saturn always gets adjusted according to the house it is in, but it never completely disappears. The dissolve is merely an illusion. It's still Saturn, but in this case, it's Saturn in the mystical spiritual Twelfth House, which just doesn't feel as solid to most people. And it's not.

Some Saturn in the Twelfth House people may very well not have that desire for the typical Saturn worlds of career gains and materialism, and yet Saturn still retains its authority. It's just different.

And similar to the Eighth House, the Twelfth House holds secrets and what is hidden, and Saturn here claims ownership of those secrets and chooses what will and won't be revealed. Saturn is the gatekeeper. Isn't this what we really need? At least as much as we need money? We need to understand the hidden, invisible world. Saturn thus comes out of the waters of chaos to teach us about these mysterious hidden worlds. Saturn is always the teacher.

Saturn in the Twelfth House is a daydreamer in the early years, a romantic in the later years. It may have been impossible to get this kid to do anything. Do homework? What? And then off to stare out the window once more. There was probably an aptitude or at least an appreciation for music and likely what they'd call an oversensitive or melancholy child. Anxious too. Their inner critic, and we all have one, was as loud as any other Saturn, and yet muffled by Twelfth House waves and poetry.

Teaching yoga or meditation may be the best job in the world for Saturn in the Twelfth House. Saturn takes the spiritual Twelfth House and brings structure to it. Yoga and meditation are both technique-based practices. There are rules (Saturn), and yet the rules are in service of something higher, including Twelfth House spiritual insight.

What else might a Saturn in the Twelfth House person do for a living? Think hypnotist. Think past-life regression therapist. Any job where you move between worlds. Also, anything having to do with water, like a sailor. Swimmer. Mapmaker. Navigator. Compass maker. Any job where you can drift and dream. Saturn doesn't become wimpy in the Twelfth House. It's as smart as ever, but it does try to take control of worlds that aren't easily controlled.

At its best, Saturn in the Twelfth House is kind, compassionate, and knows there is more to life than this physical body. Saturn in the Twelfth House will also teach compassion to others, usually without judgment. There's no ego in this placement because the Twelfth House has none. It's the house of no boundaries, no separations. Instead, we merge. This is why people with planets in their Twelfth House, including Saturn, make the best intuitives and healers—because they live half in this world and half in that world, and that world is different from ours. It is the world of spirit and the world of dreams.

At its worst, Saturn in the Twelfth House will fear everything the Twelfth House is about, all the mysteries, all the silences and secrets. It will try to control or boss around the Twelfth House wisdom rather than translate the treasures found there. The

Twelfth House can never fully be understood, not from here, not from earth. It has to breathe. It has to be. We can't just put Saturn structures all over it with a heavy hand. It must be done lightly, gently, empathically. Too much Saturn here will staunch the flow.

Saturn in the Twelfth House may also lack personal discipline. Their ambitions go down the drain, or they never had any to begin with. They start projects, and the projects disappear. What were they? Did I have any goals? Oh, well. Saturn in the Twelfth House can feel like one big sigh.

Dear Saturn in the Twelfth House, your world is an enigma to us. Please teach us what you know.

The Saturn Return

Even if you know nothing else about astrology, you may have heard about the Saturn Return. Its perilous reputation precedes it. It's when Saturn returns to its natal position in our charts, same sign, same house, same degree. Many, however, do not realize that we get two, or even three, of these, if we live long enough. Some people of course get one or none. Both my parents had died before *my* Saturn Return, and neither of them lived to experience their second one.

The sign is the astrological sign your Saturn is in (Saturn in Aries, Saturn in Taurus, Saturn in Gemini, etc.). Similarly, the degree is the degree number that Saturn is at in your birth chart, a number from zero to twenty-nine. Thus, your particular chart determines precisely when your Saturn Returns will happen.

I use words like "around" or "about" in this section because everyone's chart is different! Not everyone will have their Saturn Returns at the same ages, but around the same ages, within the span of a few years. If your Saturn is at five degrees of Cancer, of course you will have your Saturn Return before a twenty-five degree Saturn in Cancer because five comes before twenty-five!

Let's do some more simple math. Saturn remains in a sign for about two-and-half years, and there are twelve signs of the zodiac. It thus takes twenty-eight years or so for you to have your first Saturn Return, for Saturn to travel from your natal placement at the time of your birth all the way back around the wheel to your natal Saturn placement! Your second Saturn Return will occur around twenty-eight years after that and your third Saturn Return twenty-eight years after that.

Saturn, like the other planets, has periods of retrograde motion. "Retrograde" means the planets appear to be moving backward in the sky, and thus we count degrees backward instead of forward until Saturn changes course and goes direct again. This slows down our counting. Retrograde motion can last for months and affects the timing of when your exact Saturn Return will happen. It also affects how many times your particular Saturn will be hit during your returns.

Let's say your Saturn is at twenty-seven degrees Aquarius, toward the end of the sign. Saturn probably won't go from zero to twenty-seven in a straight line during that two-and-a-half-year time period that Saturn transits Aquarius. Saturn will get to a certain degree, stop, go retrograde, stop, and then go direct again, continuing to move forward through that sign until it reaches the end. This process will take months, and thus, you could have your Saturn Return more than once every twenty-eight years!

First Saturn Return: ages twenty-seven to thirty-one

Second Saturn Return: ages fifty-six to sixty

Third Saturn Return: ages eighty-four to ninety

Whether we know the astrology or not, we all experience the Saturn Return. It happens with or without our cognizance or permission. As long as we are alive, we continue to get older, and we continue to experience Saturn and the Saturn Return every twenty-eight years.

Now that we've gotten the technical stuff out of the way, let's talk about what the Saturn Return actually means. What does it symbolize? The Saturn Return means different things, of course, whether you are having your first, second, or third, but there are some general principles we can mention. I'll cover each of the Saturn Returns specifically in their own sections.

The Saturn Return is a rite of passage. It is a journey. It is a time period wherein we say goodbye to life as we have known it. We leave one land and enter another. We have to learn the new customs, new language, new ways of the people who are living in that new land, post-Saturn Return. There is the you before the Saturn Return (whichever one you are having) and the you after the Saturn Return. It's that important. It's that much of a change. It's that final. Old you, goodbye. New you, hello!

With the Saturn Return, we transition from one stage of life to another and we are supposed to grow. We are supposed to mature. We are supposed to *learn*. That's what Saturn requires of us, always. We can't take the old ways with us. The Saturn Return time period happens, and we cannot live as we have been. How we feel on the inside as well as the events of our lives on the outside will drive home this point to each of us, in very personal ways.

Areas of life that will be affected by a Saturn Return include, well, everything: family, relationships, work, career, money, health, spiritual life, home, philosophy of life. Some Saturn Return questions include: Why am I here? Did I miss anything? And some areas of life will matter more for you than someone else because our charts are different and our lives and values are different. My first Saturn Return may be more about learning how to save money and reducing debt, whereas your first Saturn Return may be about becoming a parent.

As though you are at a crossroads, the Saturn Return will ask you to choose your direction, choose your path, choose a side, make decisions about your life, and some of them will be difficult. Whatever is not working, whatever is not functioning or running smoothly like a well-oiled machine, you will have to leave those things behind or change them up dramatically!

You may walk out on a job, or you may get fired. You may leave your spouse or get married. They may leave you. You may decide that such and such habit, person, place, thing, or belief doesn't suit you anymore, doesn't suit the stage you are in whether or not you can explain why. You may become religious or leave your religion. You may decide to travel the world or leave home or return home. Unless you know the astrology, you may not realize that it's Saturn pushing you to become *you* and go on this journey of maturity, self-development, and wisdom.

So this happens to us every twenty-eight years. Think about it for a moment. Who were you at age twenty-four versus age thirty? Who were you at age forty-seven versus age fifty-seven? And if you live to be ninety, no doubt you will have grown past age eighty-two. What happened to you during those pivotal years? Are you the same person? I think not.

Even though we're all different, one thing is guaranteed about the Saturn Return: You will change. Your life on the outside, and on the inside, will change. All three of the Saturn Returns push us to wonder what we have done, what we are doing, what we will do, but this feels different at thirty, at sixty, at ninety because of what we have achieved and because of what we have lost.

Think of Saturn as a ladder. The higher you go, the greater your potential to fall, but the higher you go, the closer you get to the stars.

The First Saturn Return: The Kid

Your first Saturn Return is the journey from the end of childhood to the start of adulthood. Yes, that journey. If you are between the ages of twenty-seven and thirty reading this, then this section is especially for you.

Any astrologer will tell you it's one of the most important transits you'll ever face. The Saturn Return, the first one (the main one, some would argue) marks your passage from kid to grown-up. Welcome to the world. Many of us are still children at age twenty-six, twenty-seven, twenty-eight, twenty-nine. We need our parents. We are not yet Saturn the teacher or Saturn the builder, not really. The Saturn Return, however, makes it painfully obvious that, in certain key ways, we cannot afford to remain children any longer. My choice of the word "afford" is not an accident here because when we deal with Saturn transits, we are usually dealing with work and career (Tenth House), discipline and responsibility, and by extension, money and support.

As I type and think here, I'm reminded of the tarot card Strength, which in some decks was (and is) named *La Force*. Saturn returns to its rightful place in our birth charts, and we must restrain our many impulses, temptations, and desires to continue on as we were, as children. This takes strength.

Does something magical happen when you reach your late twenties, that Saturn Return time frame? Maybe. What converges then? This is my other Saturn Return keyword: converge. Convergence.

What was at the crossroads for you? Do you remember? If you haven't had your first Saturn Return yet, do you have a feeling of what is to come, of what choices or directions you must reckon with?

The purpose of this first Saturn Return is for Saturn to put you in your place, to root you, steady you, by seemingly doing the exact opposite: Saturn catapulting you to a brand new reality. The first

Saturn Return says: You can't be a kid anymore. Time to grow up. Time to leave home, literally or figuratively. You're like the tightrope walker who must get from here to there without falling, without breaking, and if you do fall and break, that you get back up and set the bone.

Once you reach this first Saturn Return age, the things of your younger years, teens, early twenties, just won't fit you anymore, like a sweater that's become too big or too small. Even if those things, people, places, states of mind still exist in you and around you, and many of them will because meaningful change doesn't happen overnight, you'll begin to see that too big or too small sweater as all wrong.

The more you try to hold on to the little kid inside you, the harder Saturn will shake up your world. The more you say, "Yes, I accept responsibility for my life now," which will be far more responsibility than you've ever had, the more Saturn will smooth your furrowed brow, kiss your cheek chastely, and maybe, maybe, go a bit easy on you. Saturn may even buy you a new sweater. Let me make something clear, though. That little kid inside you doesn't have to die, but instead to make room for the budding grown-up who also lives inside you now.

See, the more you follow the new rules, no matter how hard the new rules are, the easier it will be. Sounds contradictory, I know. The more you do this thing that you don't really want to do, like pay your own bills and do your own laundry and not cling to the teenage you of the past, the more Saturn will say yes, you are learning the lessons, my friend! The more you resist, the more perilous tightropes Saturn will give you to cross.

Here is an example of what life could be like as you get closer to your first Saturn Return:

You're approaching your mid-twenties. You graduated high school just a few years before, and you've been working a steady but dead-end job. Or maybe it's not a dead end at all, but you've lost interest. You're in debt because of all those free, shiny credit card offers that came in the mail. You have so much promise! And so much debt.

Here's the truth: You got stuck. Your life got stuck. And this is normal.

But let's get back to the story: You have your job, you have your debt, you have many interests probably, talents too. Maybe you paint. Maybe you're great with kids. Maybe you're good at business! Whether or not you went to college, you have youth on your side. Beauty too. If your physical and mental health are fairly good, then you have the world at your fingertips. You haven't seen thirty yet. The wilderness and wildness of childhood isn't gone forever yet. It's okay to still be somewhat foolish. In fact, it's expected.

But the years passed. You stayed in this job with no real hope of advancement or future or passion, not unless you perhaps go back to school or move to another city. It pays the bills, but otherwise, you feel your soul, breath by breath, is dying. You need a challenge. You need ambition. You need to grow! Even if you loved the job when you first started way back when, you feel the stirrings now. You want more. You want to make your wallet fat. You want to make your heart sing. You want to rejoice in a job well done. You want to feel proud of yourself.

What I'm describing here in this career example could just as easily apply to a romantic relationship that has outlived its usefulness, passion, and inspiration. It's like a loaf of bread after the expiration date. Stale. Bland. Eh. And then it starts to grow mold instead of wisdom!

Your first Saturn Return will clearly, sometimes painfully, point out to you what is not working in your life, what has to change and change *big*. Like a cell phone or computer that needs updating to the latest operating system, you also need an update, an upgrade. Some parts are broken. Some parts are just tired. Some parts still fit but need adjustment. Your life itself will create situations wherein the worn out parts get removed, get taken from you, or you find the grace and guts to walk away. Ideally, what happens is a little of both.

In this example of the dead-end job, you could wind up getting yourself fired. Maybe the boredom and frustration grabs ahold of you and you simply stop working. On the surface, you tell yourself that you're not quite ready for a big change or that you're afraid and don't know what else to do.

You tell yourself all kinds of stories, but you diligently go to work each day without actually working, until one day someone notices. That someone tells someone, and that someone tells someone else, and you get let go. At the time, you may bemoan your terrible luck until you realize that it's most likely a blessing in disguise. Through fate or because of your own subconscious desire, you are now faced with either finding a new dead-end job or finding something better and taking the Saturn challenge.

Now's your chance to commit to your life. You can find the new path that will lead you and guide you until your next Saturn Return, twenty-eight years from this point, or you might commit to an earlier way that you had to abandon or let go. No matter what you choose, Saturn comes to reorient you, and that's a nice way of putting it.

Before your first Saturn Return? Stuck. During the Saturn Return? It's like a loose tooth starting to wobble. You begin to break free of the stuck patterns that no longer serve you or at least become more aware of them. After the Saturn Return? Ideally, you paid attention and are making the required fixes. The tightrope stretches and yet grows stronger.

What is unique about this first Saturn Return?

» You are young enough to make plenty of "mistakes," and it's easier to bounce back. Youth and beauty are yours, no matter how low your self-esteem may be.

» You have your health. I know there are exceptions to this, but ideally, you have glowing, happy health on your side.

» You aren't as concerned with putting down roots yet or buying property, compared to the later years.

» You don't feel the need to have your perfect dream job yet. Society tells you it's fine to experiment. Society tells you that you have time (even if your own family disagrees). Same with true love. Maybe you'll find it now, and maybe you won't. Time is on your side, and yet the clock begins to tick. If you are female and wish to become a mother, then the ticking gets louder.

» Familial or cultural pressure could keep you feeling trapped in their idea of what you "should" do in terms of career, relationship, beliefs, your entire lifestyle.

» Parents or other family may help you financially as you learn to walk and fall and get back up again during this time. They're your safety net.

» Because you are young, you have that "whole life in front of me" mindset. Even if you are partnered and have children and many grown-up responsibilities, you feel the hope and exuberance that often dims with age and experience. And unless you have children, you simply don't have that many financial responsibilities yet. You can focus on you, your dreams.

» Because you are young, you have the illusion of endless time and endless options to travel, to go to school, flunk out of school, destroy your credit, repair your credit, destroy your life, rebuild your life. You have second chances in the decades ahead.

» Because you are young, you lack the wisdom that Saturn wants from us! You will stumble before, during, and after your Saturn Return, but that's the way it's supposed to be. The tightrope will snap. You'll fall. You'll break. You'll get stuck in the brambles below. Then Saturn in his tough-love wisdom will give you a hand and help you back on your feet.

The Second Saturn Return:
Not Dead Yet

You come home to find your husband or wife in bed with your best friend. You go to work and your job has now been filled by a younger version of you (someone probably experiencing their first Saturn Return!).

You wake up in the morning stressed about your mortgage, the car, how much the new roof on your house will cost, your children's choices, your thinning and graying hair, your health. Who you used to be. How you used to look. Was it all worth it? Is this my life? Or maybe you feel sad because you never had the house, the car, the kids, or maybe you had them and you lost them. Regret sets in and maybe even bitterness. The good news is that the second Saturn Return is good medicine for this existential station. Not dead yet.

The above scenarios could happen at any adult age, even the thinning or graying hair, but they tend to be hallmarks of the later years we call middle age or past middle age, which is the moment of the second Saturn Return, the late fifties. No one would call you elderly; although you're too old to act like a foolish kid, you're too young for the grave.

As with all the Saturn Returns, you must evaluate what *is* and what you want for your future. Stop. Think. Slow down. Yes, you do have a future, even if it doesn't feel that way. For sure, this time period will be at least occasionally marked by feelings of: Why bother? Can I really do anything new or important with my life? Old dogs, new tricks?

It's never too late for the lessons of Saturn, though, and I am certain this is the most important Saturn Return of all.

The first Saturn Return is all about leaving childhood behind, making mistakes, fixing them, and getting the first taste of real grown-up responsibility.

The third Saturn Return, which I'll address in its own section, is primarily spiritual and creative. It's also a transit of saying goodbye. Let's not mince words here. When you've hit your eighties, you're on your way out of this earthly form and moving into spirit form as the reality of old age and death is impossible to ignore like a neon billboard sign. Even if your health is good at eighty-five, you can't help but look back on your life and reflect, whereas with the first Saturn Return, you look firmly ahead.

The middle passage, or second Saturn Return, is when you can stretch your legs and see the years behind but also the years and decades to come. Late fifties. Midlife. Midlife crisis. Health crisis. What-do-I-do-with-the-next-twenty-years crisis. Did-I-waste-my-life crisis.

Retirement? Impossible, not yet, but dreaming about it. Frightened about it. Aging. Aging parents. Sick parents. Empty nest or acceptance of no biological children, not in this life. Mortality. Death feels closer. Mortgage paid off, hopefully.

Now, of course, not every second Saturn Return winner across the globe and galaxy will get sick or finish paying off a house, but these are common scenarios. Diabetes, high blood pressure, followed by the commitment to reversing both. I remember so many movies from the 1970s with that scene of a man, usually a man, buying a cherry red sports car (or having an affair) when he hits a certain age. He steps out.

For many of us, the philosophical or spiritual questions of the second Saturn Return may be the same as the first one. Where did the time go? What do I do with my life now? Do I still have time to achieve and build?

Ideally, we have achieved mastery in at least one area of life between our twenties and our fifties, and this mastery may have nothing to do with property or money or big famous careers. Maybe you self-published your spiritual autobiography or sailed around the world or healed your traumatic childhood and now you help others. Maybe you didn't heal completely but you still help others, powerful guide that you are.

The stakes are higher. It's all about the stakes. This is the time for you to make your most conscious choices. What do you want? What do you really want? You're young enough to still have another dream or two or great love in the hopper but old enough to know some dreams are out of reach. Doors close. Other doors open. And open. And open!

The areas of life that are of concern during the second Saturn Return are similar and yet different than the first Saturn Return:

» Regarding love and sex, it's not too late if you are still looking—whether you are divorced, separated, widowed, or seriously dating. I've seen friends and clients find love in their late fifties or early sixties, for the first or second time. Although the Internet has made dating all around the world possible, you are more stubborn and set in your ways than you were during your first Saturn Return. For ladies already in or entering menopause, these years can be a gateway to your most exquisite sexual pleasure and freedom. And you gentlemen have learned how to better please your partner and have staying power unavailable to your younger more hormonally charged competitors.

» You're twenty-eight years older! Some may call you older and wiser, but you may just feel over the hill. You don't have that thirty- or forty- or fifty-year-old face or body anymore, but you have a body of wisdom to share. Your outlook is that of a budding crone or elder. You're not there yet a hundred percent, but you're on your way. People listen to you, and they should. You get asked for advice. And money.

» You may feel as young as ever despite nearly sixty years on the planet. Ever notice how young people often feel old or we call them old souls? You feel younger the older you get.

» If you had children, then they are likely leading their own lives by now. You may have grandchildren. You may be helping to raise them or have an empty nest for those who became parents in their forties. If you didn't have children, then you may have complicated emotions about this. Or not. In either case, you come to terms with it. Or not.

» You have become an expert, good or great at something. Acknowledge this. Do you feel pride at all? You have valuable life experience in relationships or work or travel, achievement, art. Perhaps multiple areas. You also have likely acquired not only the previously mentioned wisdom but also property, possessions, savings. You fear losing these precious resources while also feeling burdened by them. You have invested in your life. And if you don't have these things, property, possessions, money, you may feel happily free as a bird or feel lost, without anchor or safe harbor.

» At the second Saturn Return, you will likely feel regret over the one that got away, be it person, place, thing, dream, idea. You reflect on your mortality. How many years left? How will I die? You finalize your will. You purchase a burial plot. You can joke about the end while knowing it's probably, hopefully, not around the corner.

» Health issues, physical or psychological, that you were able to ignore in younger years, come to the fore. You may be caring for sick or aging parents or dealing with the death of a parent. You may be dealing with a sick or aging partner or spouse.

» You will be thinking about a later-in-life career change or early retirement or deciding not to retire, ever. We all know that one lady or gentlemen who refuses to stop working and they probably never will! You have likely gotten serious about how you will pay your bills once the paychecks stop coming. Financial reality is impossible to ignore now, and Saturn is a saver even if you weren't.

Remember those high stakes I mentioned? I've seen many late fifties, early sixties folks undergo massive spiritual awakenings during these years.

.The stakes now aren't just work and family and love but the meaning of life, and it has a different tone than at twenty or thirty or forty or fifty.

By the time you reach your second Saturn Return, you have built a life, no matter its shape, no matter what you have. Whether you like it or not, it exists. You have built it. If you don't like it, you can still go to the hardware store and buy new wood, new tools, new plans, new paint, and rebuild. Saturn is the builder, and your spiritual life is part of this too.

Also, by this age, you know who you are. Or at least know who you are not. At its best, the second Saturn Return brings balance to your life. It's like a chessboard with all the pieces laid out for you and you ponder your next move. What choice will you make?

The Third Saturn Return: Sage Stage

You're not old, you're seasoned. Perfected wisdom. You're the Hermit card from the tarot deck. Maybe you've reached enlightenment. Even if you lived a wild life in your youth, by your third Saturn Return, you have likely learned from those wild days and become sane and sage—or at least grasped one or two of Saturn's lessons and now keep your crazy at arm's length. If your health in your seventies and eighties didn't give you a wake-up call, then your life partner or child or best friend's health did, or maybe you got a kick in the teeth from some other astrological transit. Whatever the particulars, you *are* Saturn now.

With the first Saturn Return, you were a kid, lost in the woods with a small map and bad glasses. With the second Saturn Return, the map is better, bigger print, fleshed out. You have progressive lenses, but you bought the best, and you were on your way to wisdom like a national monument in the great wide open. You were getting there, still learning, still making mistakes, figuring things out along the way.

Now? You have arrived. Crone. Elder. Respect.

Everything you've seen and done could fill a book. Or twenty books. An entire library. Teacher, master, shaman, priestess. Saturn. You may not be all-knowing, but you're damn close.

Here's one big difference from the previous Saturn Returns and decades: how you spend your daily life, how you spend your time. You may not be working at all! And yet, due to better preventative health care or medical advancement or just because some folks can't stand to sit still, some people even into their eighties keep busy, busy, busy, working or volunteering.

Even if you are still working, though, the experience and questions of the last Saturn Return are fundamentally contemplative and creative. After all this time, who are you? You're the teacher, crone, wise one now. Are you able to share it?

No matter what you do with your time, your world is slower and quieter, even if you are healthy and full of light and life. If you have family or children, then they may be looking after you, although their lives are their own, filled with work and changes and their children and goals. Consider yourself lucky if you are the respected patriarch or matriarch. Many will be in nursing homes or other assisted living.

There are other questions unique to this third Saturn Return, and for the first time, they have a finality about them because let's be honest: none of us lives forever.

What was your life about? What is your legacy? These questions are not to fill you with sorrow, and they don't have to because *now* is the time to tell your story. Tell it to anyone who will listen.

I remember emailing my maternal Uncle Joe to ask him about his parents, my great-grandparents: What were their lives like? When did they leave Russia? How religious were they?

My questions may not be your questions, but if you have an elder in your life, ask them to tell you everything they remember. They have precious stories that unless recorded will disappear. The story of where you come from is embedded, encoded in their stories.

What is unique about the third Saturn Return? Some of these may seem like ideals or impossibilities to you (or, alternately, as grim realities), but give it a few years, or decades. You'll see.

» You've won. You've beaten the odds, the years. You're still here. Not everyone gets to live this long, and that in and of itself is an accomplishment. You've loved, lost, learned, earned, spent, created. You've experienced nearly everything your soul was meant to experience. You survived!

» By this point, you are free from the pressures of youth and beauty. You have nothing to prove. Your face is your face in all its hoary glory. Of course, you want to look your best, keep those pesky hairs sprouting up in weird places under control, but there's a part of you that knows it really doesn't matter how many lines line that forehead and maybe never did. You're a soul in a body, not vice versa.

» You have no regrets. You took care of all that during your second Saturn Return. Got it out of your system. You've made peace with the past. You've forgotten (or not) and forgiven (or not). At the very least, you're less bothered. Things are as they are. You can surrender now, which is not the same thing as giving up.

» You may not be able to live on your own. If you're lucky, then you have children or other relatives or close friends to help you. Your body has slowed down, and maybe your mind too. Ideally, the doctor says you have the heart and mind and bones of a sixty-year-old, but for sure, ninety is not eighty is not seventy.

» You may have outlived your friends, your partner, your children. You may feel you've outlived even God! Mental health matters as much as physical health, so you look for ways to stay social and mentally alert. You're at risk for chronic loneliness.

» I called you the Hermit card from the tarot because I believe at the third Saturn Return, your mind is at its most flexible and insightful. You see what we cannot. You know what we don't. Even if your eyesight is absent and your knees and hips have been condemned and your mind is as holey as Swiss cheese, you are here, and we are here to listen to you.

» You are that much closer to death. Whether you find this a challenge or a gift is up to you. No doubt you have some theories about whether the soul lives forever or if there is even a soul at all. And reincarnation. Do you want to come back? You're preparing for the ultimate journey. What will it be like? Pack those bags. Confirm your flight. Wear comfortable shoes.

High Tide, Low Tide

The Saturn Return is a rite of passage.

There may be no cutting of skin or tattoo or party celebration or any visual mark or communal meal but this idea of the gate or door, portal, opening to a new world your body and soul must enter. It sounds all spiritual and fancy the way I'm presenting it to you here, and yes, you may experience it that way, but for those of us with our feet on the ground, this rite of passage is an awakening with varying degrees of rudeness, disappointment, challenge, and possibly, achievement.

The Saturn Return is a *crossroads*. We stand there at the juncture and are faced with three or four possible directions, decisions. We may stand still, paralyzed, arms at our sides, or we will cross, we will break, we will go through it, we will decide. We will take a stand. The Saturn Return *forces us* to take a stand.

Remember that Saturn rules death (along with Pluto). Although not necessarily a literal death, Saturn transits, including the Saturn Return, always include a loss and a grief process. You may mourn the childhood or innocence you can never return to or never had.

What remains after your Saturn Return is the path you are supposed to be on. Believe it even when you doubt it. Believe you are where you need to be. I know it's hard. In the process of editing this book, I am reading these very sentences over and over, and I feel them in my heart. I am here to reassure you. Find the light in the dark. And if you can't find it? Wait. Grief, they say, comes in waves. High tide, low tide.

All of this Saturn convergence and destruction is no guarantee that you'll be free of Saturn after the Saturn Return and no guarantee that your bad habits won't come back. My guess is they probably will, and you'll get another lesson and another and another. Of course, this will vary from person to person, and Saturn in the sky will continue to affect your chart as long as you are alive.

Saturn Return Magic

You can create a ritual for your entire Saturn Return year. You can construct daily or weekly meditations or journal prompts or contemplative walks dedicated to structure-loving Saturn. You can build a ritual for the month before, the week before, the day before. You can make it as big or as small as you want but I do recommend you mark it, observe it. Saturn rules time. You will make Saturn happy with such detailed attention.

Here is one option: Create a crossroads. You can draw one. Build one. Stand before one in real life. I used to live near one. I could see it from my window. Create one in your mind that you can return to again and again. See yourself there and think about your life. Where are you standing? What for? Who are you? What decisions are ahead? Sit at the juncture where the paths meet.

Earlier this year, I had a good friend visit from out of town. A local church near me was hosting a labyrinth walk and we went and we walked and walked and walked. I think we walked it five times that afternoon. At the end of the labyrinth, in the center of the room, was a chair where you could sit and wait and contemplate, although my friend sat cross-legged on the floor. After about ten minutes, maybe more, she got up and walked the maze back to the beginning.

Over the course of your Saturn Return ritual, no matter how long it lasts, the converging paths and what you need to do about them will become more clear. Slow down while under Saturn. We can feel like we want or need to speed up, that if given the chance we can outrun the lesson or our bad luck. What actually helps, though, is to slow down and be. Be there. Be with your life. Be inside it. Sit in the center.

About the Author

Aliza Einhorn, astrologer, tarot card reader, poet, and playwright, holds an MFA from the Iowa Writers' Workshop. She blogs at her website, MoonPluto Astrology, and does readings (astrology and tarot together) professionally. She also teaches metaphysical classes online and runs chat rooms for the metaphysically minded. A former New Yorker, Einhorn now resides in Florida. Visit her online at *moonplutoastrology.com*.

To Our Readers

Weiser Books, an imprint of Red Wheel/Weiser, publishes books across the entire spectrum of occult, esoteric, speculative, and New Age subjects. Our mission is to publish quality books that will make a difference in people's lives without advocating any one particular path or field of study. We value the integrity, originality, and depth of knowledge of our authors.

Our readers are our most important resource, and we appreciate your input, suggestions, and ideas about what you would like to see published.

Visit our website at *www.redwheelweiser.com* to learn about our upcoming books and free downloads, and be sure to go to *www.redwheelweiser.com/newsletter* to sign up for newsletters and exclusive offers.

You can also contact us at *info@rwwbooks.com* or at

Red Wheel/Weiser, LLC
65 Parker Street, Suite 7
Newburyport, MA 01950